GERTRUDE STEIN

LITERATURE AND LIFE: AMERICAN WRITERS

Selected list of titles in the series:

Complete list of titles in the series available from the publisher on request.

GERTRUDE STEIN

Bettina L. Knapp

A Frederick Ungar Book
CONTINUUM · NEW YORK

1990

The Continuum Publishing Company
370 Lexington Avenue
New York, NY 10017

Printed in the United States of America

Library of Congress Cataloging-in-Publication Data

Knapp, Bettina Liebowitz, 1926–
    Gertrude Stein / Bettina L. Knapp.
        p.   cm. — (Literature and life series. American writers)
    "A Frederick Ungar book."
    Includes bibliographical references.
    ISBN 0–8264–0458–8
    1. Stein, Gertrude. 1874–1946. 2. Authors, American—20th
century—Biography. I. Title. II. Series.
PS3537.T323Z67   1990
818'.5209—dc20
    [B]   89–25342
                                                                    CIP

Contents

Introduction

The mere mention of the name of Gertrude Stein immediately brings to mind "a rose is a rose is a rose" or "pigeons on the grass alas." It also recalls some of her eponyms, "the Mother Goose of Montparnasse" or the "Sibyl of Montparnasse." Visions of the apartment and studio she shared with her brother, Leo, at 27, rue de Fleurus in Paris also take shape as one imagines such giants as Picasso, Matisse, Francis Picabia, and Juan Gris gracing their home at the turn of the century. Nor must one minimize the importance of such American visitors as Sherwood Anderson, F. Scott Fitzgerald, William Carlos Williams, Virgil Thomson, and Ernest Hemingway.

Stein was an institution. She was an era unto herself—unforgettable, spectacular, revolutionary in every sense of the word. She invigorated language and refused to conform to the provisional culture of nineteenth-century America, referred to so derogatorily by Henry James as that "circumference of civilization." Europe and particularly France seemed just the right place to go at that time for inspiration and for something equally rare: freedom of expression. Furthermore, it was in the American tradition for writers to spend long periods of time abroad, as did James Fenimore Cooper, Nathaniel Hawthorne, Margaret Fuller, T. S. Eliot, Archibald MacLeish, Richard Wright, Ernest Hemingway, Henry Miller, and others.

Virtuoso that she was, Stein mocked all literary conventions: punctuation, syntax, grammar. By violating everything that was familiar to readers, she established new speech connections and remade language. Seemingly indifferent to the impression she made on the literati of her day, she forged ahead, dislocating, deconstructing, dismantling, fragmenting, and assaulting popular modes. So revolutionary was her way that T. S. Eliot, when visiting her in Paris, asked her the name of her mentor. He wanted to know who had advised her to use so many dangling participles. With pride she replied, "Henry James."

Her radical departure from nineteenth-century discourse, from logical and causal reasoning and thought processes, created a whole new approach to both writing and reading. No longer could readers remain passive recipients of whatever was narrated. Nor could they thrill to the excitement and suspense of coming events. Some were shocked and perplexed by the many repetitions and variants of these that they saw imprinted on the page; others were confused by what they considered simplistic banalities and her use of popular, everyday words and phrases intended to convey something complex. There were those who were angered by what they considered to be traps and masks hiding some esoteric knowledge; and, finally, there were readers who were frankly bored by what they considered dull and endless verbiage.

Stein knew well what she was doing. Her course was involved. First, she put the *word* through a ringer. Once cleansed of its barnacles—those nineteenth-century stale and worn appendages that had taken the very *livingness* and newness out of it—the word was reexamined and reevaluated. Genres such as the novella, novel, poetry, and theater, also went through the same severe, sometimes triturating, process. Banished was the well-made plot with its suspenseful episodes and slackening aftermaths designed to carry readers along. Gone were characterizations and highly polished texts that had once delectated the readers of Stendhal, Balzac, and Flaubert in France; of Melville and Hawthorne in the United States; of the Brontës, Thackeray, and Dickens in England. What did Stein offer instead? No plot, no representationalism, no causal sequences of events, and non-referential, therefore self-contained, movement. To add to the complexities, which Stein considered simplifications and clarifications, were the virtually infinite repetitions and their variations. No transitions. No connections. No sense of progress. Rather than espousing mimetism, Stein devalued the word to create a magical realm, an atmosphere, a landscape of her own. Unlike the surrealists, however, she was not fixated on the unconscious—at least, not consciously so. Her reality was composed of abstract temporal and spatial positions lived in a *continuous present*. Thus did she invite readers to view fragments of a life—or lives—drawn from past, present, and future time frames, each exposing continuously new elements within a character who anyway contains them *all*.

Important as well was the interdisciplinary nature of many of Stein's works, notably her short story, "Melanctha" and her verbal portraits of Picasso, Matisse, Cézanne, Apollinaire, and others. Cézanne was her guide in the writing process, she tells us in her *Autobiography of Alice B. Toklas*. From him, she learned to geometricize sensation, to do away with compositional hierarchies and the notion of a central idea as the pivotal element of a canvas or writing venture. Each segment of her novels, plays, and novellas was considered as important as the next and thus she created a kind of *text-object*. Her use of the triangle and the square was hidden within the very structure of such novellas as "Q.E.D." and "Fernhurst," and was accentuated in *Three Lives*. Her intent was to "re-create" nature through a simplification of forms right down to their basic geometric equivalents. In so doing, she developed new narrative spatial patterns within which her characters stopped, talked, or loved, while inviting readers to observe them from continuously shifting vantage points. Nothing was static, yet all was immobile—printed in the word.

From Picasso and his cubist paintings, Stein learned to emphasize still lifes and to use commonplace objects, such as potatoes or asparagus, to garnish her slim volume of poems, *Tender Buttons*. For her, however, these very same objects were also endowed with cerebral, spiritual, and sexual equivalents. Nevertheless, no defining or ordering of words in logical and understandable groupings is evident. As Picasso, Georges Braque, and Gris created their collages, so Stein generated her own reality in the word, which she viewed as a *thing* in and of itself. Be it in her poems (*Tender Buttons*), her novels, (*A Novel of Thank You*), or her plays (*Capital Capitals*), words were non-referential, non-relational, non-ideational, non-illusionist. The word replicated the essence or inherent nature of the object.

Because visual, vocal, and verbal qualities were fused in Stein's writings, she succeeded in breaking new ground by doing away with noun-referents that would have involved memory and therefore a tying to a past. Other parts of speech—adjectives, adverbs, conjunctions, and the like—were used by her to obliterate any and all of language's sign-functions. Free-flowing, her writings became so abstruse that Stein suggested relying on associational connections and internal and interlocking relationships as an indication of the person's or the object's immanence, rather than on traditional grammatical and syntactical order.

Stein may certainly be looked upon as a precursor of the French "New Novelists": Michel Butor, Alain Robbe-Grillet, Nathalie Sarraute, Marguerite Duras, and Robert Pinget. Although drastically different from one another, they were homogeneous in their desire to eradicate the nineteenth-century traditional genres. Like Stein, their disembodied characters make their plotless ways through a non-referential, non-narrative, and highly repetitive world. The abolition of chronological time and conventional spatial concepts serve further to increase the contradictory, troubling, and mysterious elements implicit in their works. The Steinian puzzles, replete in such novels as *The Making of Americans, A Long Gay Book, Many Many Women, Mrs. Reynolds,* make significations difficult to grasp. Her partial goal, like that of the "New Novelists," was to discover the secrets of that nearly mathematical order lying hidden behind the world of appearances. Other contemporary writers, such as Claude Ollier, who also treads Stein's path, seek to create an atmosphere in which the author becomes nonexistent. The world presented to the reader is embedded in a plethora of floating and non-referential descriptive details revolving around gestures, discourses, events, and souvenirs—leaving the reader thoroughly disoriented.

Is such writing to be considered alienating from society? If so, one may consider *Steinese* as having influenced not only a whole "Lost Generation," as Hemingway noted in *The Sun Also Rises,* but the "Beat Generation," such as Jack Kerouac and Allen Ginsberg. (She, however, did not indulge in drugs or in liquor, which she knew diminished the lucidity of the creative artist.) Elements of *Steinese* are also to be found in Kurt Vonnegut's works and in those of William Burroughs and others.

Stein's verbal gymnastics, as contained in *A Long Gay Book, Many Many Women,* and much of her poetry, are also reminiscent of some of the writings of Raymond Queneau, the founder of the Workshop for Potential Literature (*OLIPO*). Resorting to secret systems, self-contained and interconnecting fantasies, his computerized perimathematical fiction and poetry and ultramechanical literary works allow little room for the imagination to play.

Stein's theater may also be considered a forerunner, to a certain extent, of the works of such dramatists as Eugène Ionesco, Arthur Adamov, Fernando Arrabal, Samuel Beckett, and Harold Pinter. Her seventy-seven anti-literary and anti-theatrical plays subvert language. Humor is hard and biting. No plot, no characters, no logic in the sequence of events. No transitions. No connections. No empathy. No anthropomorphism. Actors, in such theatrical works as *What Happened, a Play, Four Saints in Three Acts,* and *Doctor Faustus Lights the Lights,* are the words themselves.

And then, there are many other delectable *things* about Stein's writings that not only keep contemporary readers enthralled but irritate them as well. And then, and then, and then—to indulge in a little *Steinese*. To quote her once again: "Also there is why is it that in this epoch the only real literary thinking has been done by a woman."[1]

Chronology

1874 Birth of Gertrude Stein, February 3, in Allegheny, Pennsylvania.

1875–78 Stein family moves to Austria and then France.

1879 Stein family moves to Baltimore.

1880 Stein family lives in Oakland.

1888 Stein's mother, Amelia, dies of cancer.

1891 Her father, Daniel Stein, dies of an apparent heart attack.

1892 Stein lives in Baltimore.

1893 Stein enters Harvard Annex (renamed Radcliffe College in 1894).

1894 Student of William James. Works in the Harvard Psychological Laboratory directed by Hugo Munsterberg.

1896 Stein's first publication, "Normal Motor Automatism," with Leon Solomons.

1897 Enrolls at Johns Hopkins Medical School.

1901 After failing four courses at Hopkins, Stein is denied her degree.

1903 Moves to Paris and shares an apartment with her brother, Leo Stein, at 27, rue de Fleurus. Writes "Q.E.D." and begins "Fernhurst."

1905   Brother and sister buy Henri Matisse's *La Femme au Chapeau*. Meets Pablo Picasso.

1906   Poses for Picasso.

1907   Alice B. Toklas and Stein meet.

1909   Alice moves into 27, rue de Fleurus. *Three Lives* is published.

1911   Completes *The Making of Americans* begun in 1902.

1912   Completes *Two: Gertrude Stein and Her Brother*. Alfred Stieglitz publishes Stein's verbal portraits "Matisse" and "Picasso" in *Camera Work*.

1913   Leo moves out of 27, rue de Fleurus.

1914   Publication of *Tender Buttons*.

1915   Stein and Toklas spend a year in Spain.

1917   Stein and Toklas return to Paris. Work for American Fund for French Wounded.

1921   Stein meets Sherwood Anderson.

1922   Meets Ernest Hemingway. Publication of *Geography and Plays*.

1925   Publication of *The Making of Americans*.

1926   Lectures at Oxford and Cambridge on "Composition as Explanation." Meets Virgil Thomson.

1929   Rents house at Bilignin, France.

1931   *Lucy Church Amiably* and *How to Write* published by *The Plain Edition* funded by Stein.

1933   Publication of *The Autobiography of Alice B. Toklas*. A best-seller. Publication of *Matisse Picasso and Gertrude Stein with Two Shorter Stories*.

1934   *Four Saints in Three Acts* premiered in Hartford and then in New York. Stein begins her lecture tour in the United States.

1936   Lectures at Oxford and Cambridge. Publication of *The Geographical History of America; or, The Relation of Human Nature to the Human Mind.*

1938   Stein and Toklas move to rue Christine. Completes *Doctor Faustus Lights the Lights.*

1939   Stein and Toklas settle at Bilignin and Culoz during World War II and the German Occupation.

1941   Publication of *Ida.*

1945   Stein and Toklas return to Paris. Publication of *Wars I Have Seen.*

1946   On July 27 Stein dies of cancer.

1947   Leo Stein dies of cancer.

1967   Toklas dies.

Part I

The Life

I feel with my eyes and it does not make any difference to
me what language I hear. I don't hear a language, I hear
tones of voices and rhythms, but with my eyes I see words
and sentences and there is for me only one language and
that is english.

—Gertrude Stein, *The Autobiography of Alice B. Toklas*

1

xxxxxxxxxxxxxxxxxxxxxxxxxxxxxxxxxxxxxxxxxxxxxxxxxxxxxxxxxxxxxxxxxxxxxx

The Exile

In 1903 Gertrude Stein left the United States to join her brother, Leo, in Paris. In the space of only a few years, the rented apartment-studio at 27, rue de Fleurus became one of the most celebrated and exclusive avant-garde salons the city—and perhaps even the world—has ever known. Writers, painters, and musicians, anyone who was anyone and even those who were no one were drawn, as metal to a magnet, to the Steins' orbit. Discussions by the tantalized, energized, inspired, even angered or insulted coterie were often explosive.

Gertrude Stein was fascinated by Paris: its tortuous streets; the Seine with its quays and bookstalls yielding the clever collector treasures of all types; the Louvre, once the home of kings; Notre Dame with its grotesque gargoyles, and its counterpart, the modern Sacré-Coeur standing in its whiteness atop Montmartre; the Latin Quarter, the home of the now-well-known "romantic" bohemian; the carefully planted and colorful Tuileries and Luxembourg Gardens; and the Eiffel Tower, constructed in 1889 as harbinger of twentieth-century engineering.

To settle in Paris was the dream of many. Stein was one of the fortunates. Moving there three years after Maurice Denis had painted his much-discussed *Hommage à Cézanne,* a canvas featuring such painters as Pierre Bonnard, Edouard Vuillard, Odilon Redon, Louis-Paul-Henri Sérusier, surrounded by their "master": and three years after the Great World Exhibition, considered a landmark in the arts because its organizers had invited the hitherto maligned Impressionists and Postimpressionists to show their work—the young American was opened to unheard-of wonders as old ways, old visionings, and old views ebbed.

Young artists were flocking to Paris even though, by 1903, Paul
Gauguin had left for the Marquesas, and van Gogh, Georges
Seurat, Alfred Sisley, Camille Pissarro, and Toulouse-Lautrec
were dead. Edgar Degas and Claude Monet were suffering eye-
sight problems and Cézanne had only three more years. Georges
Braque, Fernand Léger, and Picasso reached Paris in 1900; Wassily
Kandinsky and Umberto Boccioni in 1902; Franz Marc in 1903;
Jean Arp, Marcel Duchamp, and Constantin Brancusi in 1904;
John Marin in 1905; Gino Severini and Amedeo Modigliani in
1906. The flood tide continued with Georges Rouault, Robert
Delaunay, André Derain, Maurice de Vlaminck, and many others.

Rebellious movements in the arts were also in the offing. *Les
Fauves* (The Wild Beasts) reacted against the brilliant luminosities
of Impressionists and Postimpressionism, such as Monet, Sisley,
Renoir. *Les Fauves* was a derisive term coined to describe the vi-
olent distortions, the discordant and brash cacophony of colors
displayed by such painters as Matisse, the leader of the group,
Derain, Vlaminck, and Kees van Dongen.

Matisse's revolutionary canvases thrust aside the dominant and
popular modes of his day. His breakthrough had been inspired to
a great extent by Cézanne's *Three Bathers*. This treasured canvas
that Matisse had bought in 1899 from the art dealer Ambroise
Vollard, remained with him until he gave it to the Museum of the
City of Paris in 1936. It "sustained me spiritually in the critical
moments of my career as an artist," he wrote. "I have drawn
from it my faith and my perseverence."[1]

Cézanne's need to view the world objectively (as an object),
was instrumental in his being considered the father of the Modern Movement.[2] Going beyond Impressionistic shimmerings and
nebulous surfaces, he attempted to transform his visual perceptions into material form by discovering the structured order that
lay behind the formless and fleeting screens of color his eye observed. When giving advice to a young painter, Cézanne suggested that he "treat nature in terms of the cylinder, and the
sphere and the cone," thus reproducing its dimensionalities and
forms as simply as possible so that each "side of the object may
be directed toward a central point."[3]

Art for Cézanne was not mimesis anymore than it would be for
Matisse or Picasso—or Stein, influenced as she was by the pictorial wealth she came to experience in Paris.

Why did Stein choose to exile herself from the United States and spend nearly forty-three of her sixty-seven years in Paris? Her childhood and adolescence had been marked by pain and struggle—not by poverty or persecution (the fate of so many Jewish families who had emigrated from Europe to the United States). Stein's anxieties stemmed from the profound and searing wound she had sustained as a child from inadequate parenting. Unwittingly, she had been deprived of that very factor that creates a sense of well-being and self-worth in a child. Love and affection from her busy and self-involved mother or father were more than sparing. Lonely, thrust upon her own emotional resources, Stein's virtually sole and steady companion—her only great love throughout her adolescence—was her brother Leo, who was nearly two years her senior.

The youngest of seven children, two of whom died in infancy, Gertrude Stein was born on February 3, 1874, in Allegheny, Pennsylvania. One year later, her father, the restless Daniel Stein, having quarreled with his family, moved to Vienna with his wife, Amelia (Keyser). There he was convinced he would surely make his fortune. But the Vienna about which Daniel Stein fantasized brought neither him nor his family ease and happiness. His frequent business trips left Mrs. Stein alone and lacking affection. Frustrated and increasingly concerned about her family's precarious financial future, she became quick-tempered and allowed herself to be harsh and unfeeling, when in fact she was known to the outside world as good-hearted. At the mercy of governesses and tutors, as was the custom of the day in upper bourgeois circles, Stein, and her brothers and sisters as well, were deprived of that all-important motherly warmth.

Nor was Mrs. Stein content to remain in Vienna. By 1878 she felt so agitated that the couple decided to move the family to Paris, believing that life would be more exciting and happier there. With the exception of wonderful shopping sprees, life was no different than it had been in Vienna. The family moved to Baltimore the following year. But still in search of better business prospects, Daniel Stein again moved his family, this time to Oakland, California, where he finally settled. Fortunately, his wise investments in street railroads, real estate, and the San Francisco Stock Exchange, brought financial ease to the household. It did not, however, bring contentment. Although Stein's every whim was gratified as the youngest in the family, she was still cared for by servants, governesses, and tutors rather than her parents. She "had everything," she remarked, yet she lacked everything.

How did she view her parents, who were to become the proto-type of many of her literary figures? Her mother was pallid and passive. Her death from cancer when Stein was fourteen elicited as little sorrow from Stein as her mother had displayed affection for her. Under the circumstances, it is not surprising that an un-balanced relationship to femininity and to herself as a woman was nascent. Nor was her view of her father more positive. In her novels and autobiographies, the father image, a projection of her own, is an overbearing, authoritarian, aggressive, and egotistical figure. When Daniel Stein died of an apparent heart attack in 1891, she felt a sense of release. "There is too much fathering going on just now," she wrote, "and there is no doubt about it fathers are depressing."[4]

Other anxieties emerged, now that Stein was orphaned. There were moments when she feared for her future and her well-being. Her parents, to be sure, had been distant. Nevertheless, the sisters were provided with adequate incomes. Michael placed them in various areas. Simon, for whom Gertrude and Leo had little af-fection, remained in San Francisco: Bertha, whom they did not like any better, moved to Baltimore, as did Gertrude. Leo, who had enrolled at Harvard, accompanied them east.[5]

Gertrude and Leo, always close to one another, grew even more inseparable during these emotionally cataclysmic years. Each be-came increasingly dependent upon the other for moral and psy-chological support. Brother was the dominant force and little sister, the follower. Leo went to Harvard, while Gertrude en-rolled at the Harvard Annex in 1893 (renamed Radcliffe in 1893): he entered graduate school at Johns Hopkins, and she ma-triculated at its medical school (1897): he dropped out and left for Europe to *find himself,* whereupon she suddenly grew *bored,* failed four courses, left medical school without receiving a degree, and joined her brother in Europe (1901).[6]

Anxiety, a corrosive factor in Stein's makeup, ushered in peri-ods of profound loneliness. "Nothing is clear and nothing is sure and nothing is safe," she wrote.[7] Her brother was there, however, to assuage her pain at critical moments. Some critics have inti-mated that her relationship with Leo was psychologically incestu-ous. Others, reading into episodes contained in her novel *The*

Making of Americans, consider her relationship with her father suggestive of covert incest.[8] Whatever the interpretation of these assertions, we do know that Stein was at a loss as how to deal with her volatile emotions, how to relate to people, men or women, and how to fill the void in her heart.

That Stein was not beautiful, by the standards of the prototypal image of her day further undermined her sense of selfworth and increased her feelings of alienation. She had neither a sylphlike figure, nor was her hair attractively styled or curled. Stocky, growing plumper every day, and wearing her hair tied back or tied into a bun or knotted on top of her head, she gave an impression of extreme severity. Nor were her clothes fashionable. In fact, she seemed uncaring about her appearance. Neither feminine nor charming, her apparently unsentimental and unromantic approach to people and her highly intellectual bent did not make her popular at Radcliffe or Johns Hopkins Medical School. Did she belong? Did she want to belong? What was wrong?

Despite her physical and emotional drawbacks, Stein was respected for her fine mind. Remember that the Harvard faculty of 1894 glittered with famous men of learning: Josiah Royce, author of *The Spirit of Modern Philosophy* (1892), was looked upon as America's leading idealist; George Santayana, in his *The Sense of Beauty* (1896), considered aesthetic pleasure—as distinct from direct sensual pleasure—an irrational expression of great artistic taste; William James, known for his ground-breaking *Principles of Psychology* (1890), was perhaps one of the most influential radical empiricists in his time. Rejecting transcendent principles, he believed "pure experience" to be organized by means of "conjunctive relations," which are a matter of direct experience, as are things themselves (consciousness is only one example of "conjunctive relation" within experience).

Although Stein attended classes taught by both Royce and Santayana, James was the one she most admired and it was he who played the most active part in her intellectual formation. Enrolled in five of his courses, her marks ranging from A to B, Stein tells of an incident that seems to convey the kind of relationship James had with some—at least one—of his favorite students. Stein had gone to the opera on both the afternoon and evening prior to James's final examination. The following day, which happened to be very beautiful, Stein was not in the mood to answer the questions posed. She wrote on her paper: "Dear Professor James, I am so sorry but really I do not feel a bit like an examination paper in philosophy to-day," and left. The following day she received a postal card from her mentor that read: "Dear Miss Stein, I understand perfectly how you feel I often feel like that myself." She received the highest mark in the course.[9]

While still at Harvard, Stein did some original research under the aegis of James and Hugo Munsterberg, a specialist in psychological laboratory experimentation. Together with a graduate student, Leon Solomons, she investigated problems of attention and automatic writing. The fruit of their investigations was published in two articles in *The Psychological Review*.[10] Although a boon for the budding scientist, this kind of research work, James and Munsterberg told Stein, was not sufficient to make a name for herself in psychology. Like her mentors, she would have to earn not only a Ph.D, but a medical degree as well.

Life at Harvard was not without its emotional trials. Personality problems manifested themselves. When, for example, Stein became overly excitable during an argument she felt she was losing, she would raise her voice, believing unconsciously that her point was better taken in this manner than by logical persuasion. The psychologist Stein was unaware that those who feel the *need* to win all their arguments are masking a deep-seated inferiority complex. People considered Stein's behavior, which could be termed overcompensation for a fundamental lack of self-worth, an example of arrogance and presumptuousness. Yet, the opposite was true. The façade she erected to hide her feelings of inferiority and sense of rejection served to increase her inner tension and distress. The dichotomy between the outer and inner Stein became evident in some of her English compositions. William Vaughn Moody, a sensitive poet in his own right, in whose course Stein was enrolled, picked up the inner chaos corroding her psyche in what he considered her "extraordinary" paper, "In The Red Deeps." Because it dealt so hyperemotionally with the fear of incest and sadomasochism, he asked Stein if it had been based on a "personal experience, related in exaggerated terms," or whether it was "a study from an object [*sic*] stand point of a morbid psychological state."[11]

Other English instructors at Radcliffe were neither as perceptive as Moody nor as patient with Stein's highly *personal* writing style. Indeed, one of them, perhaps annoyed by her poor grammar and punctuation, the discontinuity of her wandering and discursive thought patterns, the many words and convoluted phrases used without apparent pith or point, write, "Your vehemence runs away with your syntax" and gave her a C for her efforts.[12]

The courses Stein took during her first two years at the Johns Hopkins University School of Medicine focused to a great extent on laboratory work. She found them to be challenging and exciting. The last two years, which emphasized "the practice and theory of medicine," bored her intensely, accounting, some critics believe, for her failure to pass four of her subjects in her last year, and then dropping out of medical school. Although one of her arguments for giving up medicine was her refusal to spend the rest of her life delivering babies, she did continue her research work in neurology for a while, eventually abandoning that subject, too. By giving up medicine she, most unexpectedly, alienated the feminists of her day, who counted on her to bring fame and power to their cause through her work as a physician. Stein seemed unperturbed. She had never been nor would become a joiner of anything—not even the feminist movement.

Now that the structured part of Stein's life had come to an end, and not having any real plans for the future, she grew understandably, apprehensive and fearful of what might be in the offing. Although she knew with certainty that she *did not* want to be a physician, she had not yet mapped out a positive course of action. Psychology continued to fascinate her, as did writing. But would these interests be sufficient to sustain her? Since she found no firm answers, Stein decided that she could profit by some time to think. Thus, she would join Leo in London. A trip to Europe with her (father-figure) brother, she reasoned, might help her decide upon her direction in life. Certainly it would broaden her views.

Brother and sister rented rooms at 20 Bloomsbury Square in the years 1902–3. Invited to Surrey to stay at the home of Mr. and Mrs. Bernard Berenson, they were delighted to meet and dialogue at length with Bertrand Russell, the art critic's brother-in-law. Years later, Berenson, in one of his gossipy moods, not only commented on Stein's girth, but on her unfeminine ways: he was repelled by the fact that after sunbathing and perspiring she remained in the same clothes. Most offensive to him was the casual manner in which she and her brother handled his precious books.[13]

Back in London and fascinated with the British Museum where she spent her days reading, Stein nevertheless decided that the climate was too damp and returned to New York. She moved in with her friend Mabel Weeks, also a Radcliffe graduate, and two other young women. She would not only allow herself more time to think about her future career, but would also try to understand herself ever more deeply, to fathom what she had kept secret for a period of time and would continue to hide from the outside world. For some, her secret was readily perceptible, given her masculine demeanor.

That Stein was a lesbian at a time when such proclivities were looked upon askance, increased her already-powerful sense of rejection and alienation. What made matters worse was her inability to cope with the pain she was suffering. She was in love with a woman, but rather than allow her feelings to emerge, she repressed them. Secretive and puritanical, the fear of becoming a social pariah was very real. She needed to find an escape, some way of alleviating the trauma she was experiencing. To verbalize her feelings was a possibility: writing them out might serve to lighten and enlighten those dark and massive agglomerations within her psyche. To this end, she made a mental outline of a novelette that was to be known as "Q.E.D." (*Quod Erat Demonstrandum* or Things as They Are). It related a love affair and its aftermath—a fictionalized version of the lesbian triangle in which Stein had been a participant and a loser—and the still-unhealed and smarting wounds of which she had been and still was a victim.

Leo, at loose ends after his sister's departure for New York, went to Paris. Also without a firm career commitment, but with perception and sensitivity as well as a great deal of knowledge of history, philosophy, biology, and art history, he decided to devote his energies to becoming a painter. To this end, he divided his time between the Louvre, art exhibits, and the small galleries peppering Montmartre and the Left Bank. To give structure and discipline to his existence and to familiarize himself with all the aspects of his future profession, he enrolled at the celebrated Académie Julian.

Leo rented a modest studio and pavillion at 27, rue de Fleurus on the Left Bank, near the Boulevard Raspail and the Luxembourg Gardens. On his walls he hung, among other works, a canvas by Wilson Steer, the English Postimpressionist and some of the Japanese block prints and paintings he had collected during and after his trip to the Orient (1895). There was no doubt that Leo had an eye for quality. He also had perception. The thought of being surrounded by and owning works he loved to look at filled him with a sense of pride and joy. Perhaps this accounted for the immediacy of his response to Berenson's suggestion that he go to Ambroise Vollard's gallery on the rue Lafitte and look at some of the works by the little-known painter, Paul Cézanne. So impressed was Leo with the canvases Vollard showed him that he decided to study the "master's" works in depth, while also pursuing his own career as a painter.

After spending the summer of 1903 vacationing with her brother in North Africa, Spain, and Italy, Stein takes up residence with Leo at 27, rue de Fleurus. This momentous decision, though she was unaware of it, changed the course of her life. This address was to remain her home until 1938 (when the owner wanted the apartment for his soon-to-be-married son), whereupon she moved to 5, rue de Christine.

In Paris in 1903, Stein put the finishing touches on "Q.E.D." Traditional in form, but perhaps shocking to many at the time both because of the subject matter and the autobiographical details concerning her unrequited love, she decided to secrete it in a cabinet and not seek its publication. Her passion for May Bookstaver, nonetheless, was real and abrasive. May was one of a group of women graduates from Smith and Bryn Mawr whom Stein had met and with whom she had become friendly during her last years at Johns Hopkins. "Q.E.D." was published only after Stein's death.

Even after the completion of "Q.E.D." Stein's gaping wound resulting from her unhappy love affair with May had not yet healed. The best medicine to assuage the hurt, she reasoned, was to set her hand to the grindstone and pursue the writing of another work, as love object and as therapy. "Fernhurst," a novella, was to fictionalize a lesbian relationship in a relatively conventional style. What made the lesbian focus even more risqué in the author's mind was not simply the exploration of the subject, but its ramifications in the heterosexual world. That the events upon which Stein based her work had taken place on the very proper and prestigious women's college at Bryn Mawr where "immoral" activities were rampant, but enfolded behind closed doors, led her to change the location of the narration.

The facts upon which Stein based "Fernhurst" are as follows: Carey Thomas, dean of Bryn Mawr, champion of women's rights, but also an authoritarian person, was in love with her protégée, the timid, retiring, but most brilliant member of the faculty, Mary Gwinn. When the young, married, and Harvard-trained Alfred Hodder came to teach at Bryn Mawr, he and Mary fell in love. The plot thickens. Its unraveling in reality and as imprinted in "Fernhurst" will be discussed in the following chapter.

Surprisingly enough, although the happenings at Bryn Mawr were hushed, they seemed to have been common knowledge. From Bertrand Russell, Stein learned that when he had been invited to lecture at Bryn Mawr in 1896, he had been told about the Hodder-Gwinn affair. Perhaps even more of a coincidence was the fact that Dean Carey Thomas was the cousin of both his wife, Alys, and his sister-in-law, Mary Berenson.[14]

That Stein had been able to verbalize her seemingly infinite hunger for affection and love in "Q.E.D." and in "Fernhurst" had helped her. Other factors also played a significant role in alleviating her painful psychological confusion and her lack of self-confidence. Residing in Paris, fertile field for the arts, and accompanying her brother to museums, art galleries, studios, and curio shops, helped to broaden her horizons. The sciences, which had been Stein's focus until now, yielded their preeminence to the world of the painter and the writer. Having left her native surroundings, which she considered a paradigm of traditionalism, and her friends, whom she had relied upon to a certain extent for emotional support, Stein found herself becoming more and more dependent upon her brother, intellectually as well as psychologically. Whether or not Leo was aware of his sister's sexual anomaly is debatable: that they discussed sexual matters is known.

Detached and distanced from everything she had known, and inspired by the novelty and excitement generated by the new and creative trends in the arts in Paris at the turn of the century, the exile's road meant striking out anew. Displacement became a rerooting.

One of the things that I have liked all these years is to be surrounded by people who know no english. It has left me more intensely alone with my eyes and my english. I do not know if it would have been possible to have english be so all in all to me otherwise. And they none of them could read a word I wrote, most of them did not even know that I did write. No. I like living with so very many people and being all alone with english and myself.[15]

Settled into a new routine, Stein and her brother spent long hours going at what they referred to as "junking" expeditions: buying Japanese prints, paintings, etchings, and drawings by artists whose works they loved. Soon, among their possessions could be found works by Renoir—Leo admired him immensely because of his "gift of color": Eugène Delacroix, "the greatest French painter of this century": Toulouse-Lautrec's *Le Divan;* Gauguin's *Three Tahitians:* Cézanne's figure compositions of his *Bathers.*[16]

As art collectors, the Steins—and especially Leo—were ground breakers. A perceptive critic, he wrote that he admired Cézanne for his "great mind . . . perfect concentration, and great control" as well as for the "vital intensity" with which he rendered mass, that "remorseless intensity," that "unending gripping of form." He considered each of his canvases a "battlefield and a victory."[17]

The year 1905 was one to remember for the Steins. It marked one of their monumental purchases: Cézanne's *Portrait of Mme Cézanne.*[18] Although Stein did not have her brother's expertise in matters of art, she did have a discerning eye and was intuitive. Important as well was her extraordinary analytical sense that empowered her to draw and absorb line, texture, rhythm, and form from the canvases she studied, and transform this information into the word.

Up to this time, Stein had accepted without question her brother's opinions concerning art. After having lived in Paris for two years, traveling to Italy during the summer months, she had learned so much that she felt more sure of herself in matters of art. Not only did she begin to explore the artist's scene on her own, but, even more significant, she started to rely upon her own reactions (aesthetic, emotional, and intellectual) to certain paintings and pieces of sculpture. Her approach to art in general, and to Cézanne's paintings in particular, was personal and subjective. Interestingly, her reasons for admiring Cézanne's canvases were antipodal to those of her brother: Leo viewed Cézanne's paintings as evolving naturally from the works of Andrea Mantegna (*Crucifixion*) and other Italian quattrocento painters, their simplified forms and illustrative needs subordinated to compositional matters; Stein, on the other hand, looked upon Cézanne's compositional value as utterly revolutionary and not inherited from past masters, because the Frenchman's sense of "realism" transcended the reality of the objects depicted. Even more crucial to Stein was

the fact that the *center* for Cézanne was no longer an organizing
principle, nor was the limiting notion of the *frame.* Everything
that was shaped, formed, and colored on a canvas was important:
not one object more than another.

Years later, Stein remarked in an interview in 1946:

Cézanne ... gave me a new feeling about composition. ... I was obsessed by this idea of composition. ... It was not solely the realism of
characters but the realism of the composition which was the important
thing. ... This ... had not been conceived as a reality until I came along,
but I got it largely from Cézanne. Flaubert ... too, had a little of the
feeling about this thing, but they none of them conceived it as an entity,
no more than any painter had done other than Cézanne.[19]

What, for Stein, had Cézanne achieved in his canvases? A rejection of hieratic and hierarchical values, moods, structures, and
meanings—the very fundaments of Western philosophy that she
felt impeded clarity of observation. "I believe in reality," she
wrote, "as Cézanne or Caliban believes in it. ... Always and
always."[20]

Because Stein took Cézanne's work so seriously, its influence
on her next work, *Three Lives,* is easily explained. In the three
novellas in this volume, each of which revolves around a servant
girl—"The Good Anna," "Melanctha," "The Gentle Lena"—
Stein transmuted into words what Cézanne had delineated in his
later paintings: a noncentered and nonframed reality. His new vision of nature and of the world of phenomena, his decentralized
thematics and spatial relationships, his geometric structurations,
all were, for Stein, marks of his genius.

On the literary side, mention must also be made of Stein's debt
to Gustave Flaubert. His short story, *"Un Coeur simple"* (A Simple Heart), she claimed, was also instrumental in the fashioning
of her writing style at the time. She admired his use of understate-
ment of narrative discourse, but mostly his concern for the *le mot
juste:* that single word that would exactly convey the author's
idea, feeling, and aesthetic values.

Unlike "Q.E.D." or "Fernhurst," "Melanctha," the most innovative of the tales included in *Three Lives,* is devoid of a "center." In transliterating Cézanne's advice to painters in her writing,
all events, tensions, anguishes in "Melanctha" were "distrib-
uted" equally throughout the novella, thus eliminating climaxes

and sequential episodes.[21] Neither does a single idea take shape in the narrative around which others gravitate, nor does one approach to characters or events prevail over another any more than one point of view assumes greater importance than the previous one. Every aspect is significant, Stein believed. What was of import was the manner in which the reactions to them were apprehended: the imaginings and emotional involvements between characters, the rhythms of the sentences and phrases, and, especially the tonality and accent of the voices at particular junctures. Most innovative on Stein's part at this time was her stylized use of repetition in her exploration and building of personality types. That she used black cant throughout her story about black Americans was also arresting.

Because of Stein's revolutionary approach to writing, *Three Lives* appealed to very few in her entourage. The open-minded Sarah Stein, Michael's wife, was perhaps one of the few who reacted enthusiastically to her work. Leo did not. Was his negative response to his sister's writing based strictly on a lack of appreciation of her avant-garde techniques? Or were his views tinged with sibling rivalry? Perhaps most disconcerting to Leo was his sister's perseverance and self-discipline, as well as the fact that she had branched out on her own, developing her own views on art and literature, and no longer paid homage to his as she had in the past. Would she remain his disciple? Stein, on the other hand, who still doted on her brother, was deeply saddened by his reaction.

Gaining in self-confidence, rather than waxing in despair, Stein decided to begin a novel: *The Making of Americans*. This innovative volume of nearly one thousand pages, begun in 1902, was completed in 1911, but not published until 1925. Again, Stein followed the Cézanne aesthetic: decentralized structurally speaking, it explores the nature and impact of disastrous marriages, unhappy love affairs, neglected and abused children, and incipient or disguised lesbianism. These themes are analyzed in terms of their effects upon the participants (individuals and groups of people) involved in an agglomeration of meandering sequences in continuously expanding relationships. Rambling and unwieldy, *The Making of Americans* nevertheless fascinates as a literary experiment.

Because Leo was forever derogating or merely overlooking his sister's literary attempts, bitterness and resentment grew within her. Still, it was repressed. She would bide her time. Leo, the surrogate *father,* was still in charge, she reasoned. He had not yet learned to appreciate or to accept his daughter/sister's talents. The warmth and understanding for which she yearned was no longer being fed by him, nor did she now need it so urgently to survive. She was passing into another stage of development: no longer passive, loving, accepting, and clinging to what could be called a mirror image of her brother's fantasies, she *knew* inside that she was on the right track. Remaining silent on the subject, however, she allowed life—at least on the outside—to pursue its course. Brother and sister continued purchasing painting upon painting, frequently inviting the artists to their home. Stein still benefited from Leo's knowledge of the arts and from the new contacts their collecting brought them. An avid learner when passionate about something, Stein absorbed fresh views, storing up these riches in her inner armory for future use.

With the purchase of Matisse's *Women with the Hat,* one of the most spectacular paintings to have graced the Salon d'Automne (October 18, 1905), the Steins made their reputation as great art collectors of the avant-garde. The Matisse canvas had been mocked and derided because of what contemporary art critics considered its primitive display of brash colorations and distorted and crude lines, but this did not discourage the Steins from buying his works. Other purchases were quick to follow: *Bonheur de vivre* (1906), *Blue Nude* (1907), *Landscape, Collioure* (1904–5), *Margot* (1907), *Music* (1907), and a sculpture, *The Slave* (1903–4). "I was alone in recognizing these two [Matisse and Picasso] as the two important men," Leo wrote perhaps boastfully.[22] Leo, however, neglected to mention that his brother, Michael, and his wife, Sarah, had also moved to Paris in 1903, settling at 58, rue Madame, not too far from Leo and his sister, and that they, too, had become devotees of Matisse and collectors of his paintings and those of other contemporary masters.

Matisse became friendly with the four Steins, visiting them in their respective homes. He would arrive at 27, rue de Fleurus with some of his friends on Saturdays—the day the Steins reserved for their gatherings. Stein later remarked that he had been the one responsible to a great extent for the now-famous get-togethers that became the talk of the avant-garde in Paris. It was, however, Leo who held court, speaking so knowledgeably on matters of art, while his sister, listened half-hidden in a corner of the room, giving the impression of a timid presence in her own home.

Leo found Matisse to be highly intuitive and intelligent; Stein, on the other hand, although admiring the painter's tremendous capacity for work, in time became critical of his approach to art. That he was a genius, she never denied. What she disliked about Matisse was his inflexibility: he was "unreasonable" and closed to new ideas, thus suffering from a "singular kind of blindness." His lack of vision, she felt, served to diminish his understanding of certain problems in the pictorial domain, thus encouraging him to hold on to *his* central idea of himself and his art. Perhaps more detrimental, in her view, was the omission of opposition or "contradiction" in Matisse's later canvases. In the old days, she intimated, when attacked by his enemies, he fought back. Now that he had a following, struggle and fight disappeared from his work.

What Stein also found offensive in Matisse's canvases was what she termed his "brutal egotism in his not changing his prices." Although she should have understood that the more popular he became, the higher the prices he could command for his paintings, she reasoned differently. Stein felt that because she and her brother had been among his earliest patrons, he should have retained his old prices for them. Not a value judgment of Matisse's art, her position revealed instead a heretofore little-known side of Stein: she could be petty and vindictive. Stein knew, moreover, that in 1909 Matisse had signed a contract with the Bernheim-Jeune gallery and no longer had the freedom to sell to individuals. The gallery set the prices; it was its responsibility to sell the paintings, and no longer the artist's. By 1915 Stein had sold all of her Matisses. Like a petulant and self-centered child, she showed little discernment or compassion: indeed, psychologically, Stein was in many ways still the little girl.

Although brother and sister no longer saw eye to eye on matters artistic, it must be noted that Leo's interest in Matisse also began diminishing. Picasso was Leo's latest enthusiasm. Perhaps the Steins' newfound fascination for Picasso was also a factor in their decreasing regard for Matisse. That Picasso and Matisse did not like each other, from the time of their first meeting at the Steins, is evident from the latter's utterance: "North Pole. South Pole."[23]

Stein first saw Picasso's work at Clovis Sagot's small shop on the rue Lafitte, near Notre-Dame-de-Lorette. Despite his sister's objections, Leo bought *Young Girl with a Basket of Flowers* (1905). Although the stories brother and sister later related concerning the purchase of Picasso's paintings are at variance, there is agreement on the part of both that Stein disliked the Spaniard's canvases. She protested to her brother: "I hated that picture": the unformed figure of an adolescent, the black hair in sharp contrast to the flaming red flowers, the ugly legs with "feet like a monkey's."[24] According to Leo, *Young Girl with a Basket of Flowers* was his second Picasso purchase after *The Acrobat's Family with a Monkey*, one of the artist's great works. Picasso was "a genius of very considerable magnitude," Leo wrote, "and one of the most notable draughtsmen living."[25]

Stein's first impression of Picasso's canvases was negative. She soon veered to the opposite extreme, however, becoming intrigued, beguiled, and finally totally absorbed by Picasso's genius and his prophetic vision. Seeing Picasso at work in his studio on the rue Ravignan in Montmartre, she came to realize that he was a man *possessed* by his work.

The building in which the painter lived, the "Bateau Lavoir" (so named because it looked like a laundry boat), was in a state of extreme dilapidation. The studio itself was sparsely furnished with broken-down odds and ends—tables, chairs, a couch used as a bed, a pot-bellied stove—and canvases and drawings all about. The Steins were more impressed than ever and purchased as many drawings and paintings from his Blue and Rose Periods as they could afford—including the famous *Boy Leading a Horse*.

In her volume on *Picasso* (1938), Stein wrote:

One must never forget that the reality of the twentieth century is not the reality of the nineteenth century, not at all and Picasso was the only one in painting who felt it, the only one. More and more the struggle to express it intensified. Matisse and all the others saw the twentieth century with their eyes, but they saw the reality of the nineteenth century. Picasso was the only one in painting who saw the twentieth century with his eyes and saw its reality, and consequently his struggle was terrifying, terrifying for himself and for the others, because he had nothing to help him, the past did not help him, nor the present, he had to do it all alone.[26]

Picasso was reciprocally fascinated by Stein. He who rarely, if ever, worked from a model, broke a precedent by asking her to pose for him. But for some strange reason, the eighty or ninety sittings that took place during the winter of 1905–6 left Picasso dissatisfied. There was an obstacle that he seemed unable to surmount. Summer was drawing near and painter and writer were due to leave Paris. Stein and her brother would spend the summer at Fiesole; Picasso was to return to Spain. Before leaving, however, Picasso attended an exhibit of pre-Roman Iberian sculpture at the Louvre. The archetypal masklike images he saw impressed themselves deeply upon his psyche. No sooner had he arrived in Spain than he began immersing himself in the harshness and starkness of the Catalan highlands. There, he worked with furor and intensity until he felt he had found what he had lost in citified Montmartre: his own primitiveness. Such enrichment enabled him to endow his images with universal and mythic motifs while also, paradoxically, revealing a personal and unique dimension of his own.[27] Upon his return to Paris, he was a man renewed. He *knew* he had solved the problem of the unfinished Stein portrait: the difficulty had resided in concretizing the *essence* of her being, those intangible qualities so deeply embedded in her face. Divesting the canvas of mimesis and of abstraction, Picasso concentrated on volume, creating for the first time a singular masklike face, angular nose, sharply etched mouth, and strangely piercing eyes that seemed to look out upon the world from unlimited archetypal depths.[28] Picasso knew that the face's very "non-resemblance" had helped him to capture the ineffable on canvas.

Stein was thrilled with the results. Leo was not. The face's angular lines—a forerunner of what he would later label Picasso's "Cubist funny business"—were not acceptable to him. Others, when visiting 27, rue de Fleurus, frowned at what they saw. It did not resemble Stein, they commented, to which Picasso countered with what has become his famous remark: "She will."[29]

Gertrude's friendship with Picasso lasted for over four decades (there were quarrels, but of a minor nature, revolving around the bruised ego of one or the other). Not only was her admiration based on his work and the lively discourse between them, but, according to Stein, his canvases influenced her writing style.

I was alone at this time in understanding him, perhaps because I was expressing the same thing in literature, perhaps because I was an American and, as I say, Spaniards and Americans have a kind of understanding of things which is the same.[30]

Because the mask in Picasso's portrait of Stein took on the power of both an icon and a "thing," it could be said that he was in the process of developing a new *iconography* which would depict reality so powerfully that it would take on aesthetic importance, becoming as significant as the figures and objects within the composition. In time his iconographic reality was to become the primary element out of which the canvas was born. It comes as no surprise to learn that, after completion of Stein's portrait, Picasso began a series of studies that led to *The Demoiselles from Avignon* (1907).[31]

Picasso was en route to cubism. So was Stein, who began broaching literary questions in a similar manner. Her analytical approach to his iconography resulted perhaps from a kind of absorption in the pictorial problems with which he was dealing at the time. Still very much of the psychologist, Stein was also fascinated by the painter's struggle with his volatile personality, his drastically alternating moods, and his unconscious fear of betraying his inner flame.[32] He was in some ways, she noted, like Basarof (a character in Turgenev's *Fathers and Sons*). There is both "reality and arrogance" in the Basarof type; "the combination makes them not susceptible of reality in others." Persons of this kind are given to fanaticism based on some "mystic idea" that finally compels them to reject "their experience ... it may make them aesthetic visionaries as Raymond [Duncan] & (I hope not) Pablo. Pablo may be saved by the intensity of his actual aesthetic experience, if he can hold to that he will go on." These people are "not slow they are blind, they are facile they learn really easily, but they are blind. Pablo's instinct is right, he does not wish to slow himself but to concentrate himself." His control over his impulses will save him, she predicted, rectifying and channeling his incredible creativity by dominating both his extreme sexuality and his propensity for esthetic mysticism. Contradiction and struggle will always pervade that tempestuous temperament of his.[33]

Parallel to Picasso, Stein was slowly developing her own personal iconography, thus enabling her to articulate *her* reality. Her new verbal aesthetic cannot be compared to Picasso's pictorial icons, and her writing does not attempt to take on its masklike and angular qualities, but her inclination toward "diagrammatic characterization," pointed to a predilection or an identification with his method of portraiture. As Leon Katz stated: "Just as Iberian stone head or African mask were on occasion the basis for Picasso's new iconography, which he then translated into a new formal vocabulary, so diagrammatic psychological relations became Gertrude's essential vocabulary; and relational contexts, even more than the characters described, became the 'objects' out of which she composed her novel."[34]

I was very much struck at this period, when cubism was a little more developed with the way Picasso could put *objects* together and make a photograph of them. I have kept one of them, and by the force of his vision it was not necessary that he paint the picture. To have brought the objects together already changed them to other things, not to another picture but to something else, to things as Picasso saw them.[35]

As Stein attempted to depict character and event diagrammatically, her vocabulary became increasingly controlled and cerebral. Occurrences and characters were looked upon as "objects" out of which she formed, molded, and created whatever was included in her writings, particularly in *The Making of Americans*. Identifying with the brutality and ugliness she saw in Picasso's paintings, she lauded his *struggle:* every great innovator must undergo this catalytic force in order to give birth to the new. Struggle is seminal: it helps give birth to image, idea, and word; it is instrumental in assisting the gestation period and in developing keenness of thought, psychological awareness, and body sensitivity. During the process, struggle serves to cut and bruise body and soul, as happens during birth—both being acts of creation. To reject the old and bring in the new engenders chaos, struggle, force, energy, power—cruelty. Picasso said, Stein noted:

he who created a thing is forced to make it ugly. In the effort to create the intensity and the struggle to create this intensity, the result always produces a certain ugliness, those who follow can make of this thing a beautiful thing because they know what they are doing, the thing having already been invented, but the inventor because he does not know what he is going to invent inevitably the thing he makes must have its ugliness.[36]

Picasso, Matisse, and herself alongside the two masters were the "ugly giants," the makers of great art.[37]

As *struggle* was Picasso's byword, so was it Stein's. She understood only too well the disturbing, perplexing, and complicated nature of Picasso's conflicts since she was experiencing similar anxieties and divisiveness when attempting to fathom the "real meaning" of her art. In Stein's portrait of "Picasso" (1909), her identification with his contending polarities becomes evident:

Something had been coming out of him, certainly it had been coming out of him, certainly it was something, certainly it had been coming out of him and it had meaning, a charming meaning, a solid meaning, a struggling meaning, a clear meaning.[38]

Stein's intense and progressively powerful search to discover, hold, and verbally re-create the essence of the painter and his work via her powerful and rhythmic use of repetition is spellbinding. By varying her focus ever so slightly throughout her composition, she succeeded in mapping out her own innovative direction. During the course of her verbal trajectory, she geometricized configurations by way of repetition, while at the same time, she fragmented and redefined her three-dimensional subjects and objects, in an attempt to depict them simultaneously on a variety of interlocking planes.[39]

Her need to create a reality in words, as Picasso had done pictorially, intensified her search to understand better Picasso's "relation to the object." Differences, of course, existed between their temperaments, needs, styles, and solutions to the artistic problems facing them. Whereas Picasso focused on *objects* as concrete phenomena existing in the visible world, Stein's interest lay in the *humanization* of the object. Both Picasso and Stein, each in his and her domain, were concerned with the artist's ability to develop the potential of the object as object, be it in the painting's composition or articulated in the written word.

Stein's quest compels her to banish logic, verisimilitude, and mimesis from her verbal constructs. "To kill the nineteenth century" was one of her goals. Although intimating that solutions are not eternal and problems not really solvable, Stein reiterates again and again her belief that the artist should concentrate on the object. When developed through its own iconographic vocabulary to the realization of its potential, it becomes the very *object* of the painting or the written work.[40]

Although Stein was evolving as a writer and deepening her vision of art, she was still struggling in her attempt to impress her own literary stamp on the world. In this vein, she began writing a series of extraordinary portraits of "Picasso," "Cézanne," and

"Matisse."[41] Her goal was to extract and then convey in the word the essence of their creativity and their temperament. What she noted about Picasso, was, interestingly, applicable to her: "He alone amongst the painters did not have the problem of expressing the truths that all the world can see but the truths that he alone can see and that is not the world the world recognizes as the world."[42]

The dismemberment of syntax, the fragmentation of ideas, the disembodiment of images, and the use of run-on sentences, which was the method she adopted in her literary portraits, made them difficult to understand at first reading. Even after absorption of the fruit of her thought and programmatic style, it must be conceded that her work was not common sharing. Her portraits were rejected by the publishers to whom Stein showed them; undaunted, she herself subsidized the publication of her writings.

Despite the fact that her verbalizations were different and difficult to fathom, personality-wise, Stein intrigued and fascinated strangers and friends alike. For example, the first time Picasso saw her, before they had even met, it was from a distance. Her appearance so impressed him that he was determined from that moment to paint her portrait. The energy she generated as she talked excited the picture dealer Ambroise Vollard:

There is nothing more lively, more fascinating than her conversation. Her eyes sparkle with intelligence. Their expression at times is mocking, but the mockery is tempered with indulgence: if a spice of it creeps into her speech, it is rounded off by a gay laugh at her own expense.[43]

Vollard also made mention of her unusual dress, which some considered outlandish and ridiculous, others grotesque:

of coarse velveteen, her sandals with leather straps, and her general air of simplicity, one would take her at first sight for a housewife whose horizon is restricted to her dealings with the greengrocer, the dairyman and the rest. But you have only to encounter her glance to perceive in Miss Stein something far beyond the ordinary *bourgeoise*. The vivacity of her glance betrays the observer, the investigator whom nothing escapes. Yet one cannot withhold one's confidence from her, so disarming is the laugh she seems constantly to turn against herself.[44]

Passionately devoted to the arts, Stein was also focused on her own comforts. She had settled into a routine that she would not vary, and she adopted a way of life that was congenial to her temperament. Because she found the night hours propitious to creativity, it was her custom to sit at the Florentine table in her studio and there, surrounded by spectacular works of art, write undisturbed for long hours at a stretch. Understandably, she slept late into the day: "I never get up early I get up as late as possible . . . and no one ever wakes me."[45]

Stein continued to preoccupy herself not only with objects as human beings—that is, as personality types—but increasingly with stylistic innovations. In *A Long Gay Book,* which Stein worked on until 1912, she sought to list as many varieties of human personality types as possible. The result was less than felicitous. Although uninspiring and tedious, it was in this novel that Stein imprinted the striking and now-famous sentence: "A day that is a day is a day," later transformed in "Sacred Emily" into "Rose is a rose is a rose is a rose".[46]

Equally uninteresting and repetitious is her diagrammatically conceived novel, *Many Many Women* (1911–12), consisting of analyses of groups of people. Both *A Long Gay Book* and *Many Many Women,* along with other works of the period, must be considered as so many exercises that Stein was putting herself through prior to the formulation of her own aesthetic. The breakthrough from conventional form to the discovery of a new and personal verbal iconography became apparent in a volume of poems, *Tender Buttons.*

Focusing her attention in *Tender Buttons* on an *object,* be it "A Red Stamp," "Red Roses," or "Asparagus," *it* became the *object* of her composition. Not only did such an iconographic approach trigger her imagination, but it also accounted for the breadth and scope of the associations resulting from the confrontation between her observing eye and the material object. The dynamism aroused by such eye contact between the human and the nonhuman world affected the manner in which the words themselves took their form and their placement on the page. Object, then, became text, pretext, and context.

Also significant in *Tender Buttons* is Stein's tripartite structuring of the volume. The headings, "Objects," "Food," and "Rooms," are the substance out of which the disparate poems will be molded, shaped, and styled. They will also function as a device enabling her to further her exploration of semantic relationships existing between the individual objects (still lifes)—that is, the poems themselves and the names awarded each of them. Stein was, in effect, performing on a verbal level what cubist painters, namely Picasso and Braque, were accomplishing on canvas.

Arresting as well is her choice of the oxymoron for the title: *Tender Buttons*. The word *Buttons* lends an energetic as well as a relatively secure quality to the image. Their circular iconicity suggests continuity, a mandala, a visual meditative device insuring deeper penetration of the object of his or her scrutiny, while also conveying feelings of serenity. Because *Tender* suggests an emotional, therefore, volatile involvement, it lends a qualitative approach to space. Thus is Stein able to present the objects in question from a variety of angles and not merely from a single, fixed, static point of view. The stable and the disparate are implicit in the title, and each of the poems, as well as the tripartite division of the volume itself, is endowed with compositional value.

Other factors also participate in the uniqueness of *Tender Buttons* (see chapter 4). Movement, for example, is not only made rhythmic by the many near repetitions, juxtapositions, and continuous ambiguities in the poems themselves, but also by the floating qualities resulting from such syntactical devices and techniques. In addition to the formation and meaning of the words themselves, Stein's contiguous placement of them on the sheet of paper activated, she believed, energy charges within the letters that form the word, which then impact on the other words of the text, thus creating ideogrammatic, associational, and melodic texts. It is also worth noting—and this occurs in certain cabalistic writings—that as each black sign is imprinted on the blank sheet of paper, thus bringing together certain letters (or symbols) used in the formation of words, unknown and mysterious factors also come into play, as if by their own volition words seem to flow into sentences and paragraphs.

Arduous and unrelenting work was required in the putting together of *Tender Buttons*. To create a scene with few and sometimes no nouns, which was Stein's intention, while also divesting the remaining words of their conventional meaning, was to jolt readers out of their lethargically secure logical approach and open them up to the object/person or object/event in a wholly new manner: "I struggled I struggled desperately with the recreation and the avoidance of nouns as nouns and yet poetry being poetry nouns are nouns."

Like the musical compositions of Arnold Schoenberg (1874–1951), Stein's works also were divested of a sense of repose. Because he viewed black and white keys not as neighbors, but as separate entities (giving sharps and flats the same value as any other note in the scale), Schoenberg eliminated moments of harmonic calm, thus creating a kind of restlessness. His innovations in turn inspired Anton Webern (1883–1945) and Alban Berg (1885–1935) to probe more deeply pure beauty of tone in and of itself. Later, Karlheinz Stockhausen (1928–) went even further with his serial and electronic techniques, emphasizing free rhythms, tonal repetition, dissonance, and percussive effects.

Stein's syntactical and grammatical experimentation was not only difficult but hazardous. How would people react to such a technique ideationally? Would they resent her cubistlike fragmentation, the breaking up and destruction of what they had believed to be whole and viewed as a unit? Would their intelligence be offended? their senses aroused? affected? or would they just cast the book aside?

Other French writers had also experimented with syntax, grammar, and verbal iconography. Among them was the warmhearted and ebullient Guillaume Apollinaire who was also, in Stein's words, an "extraordinarily brilliant" conversationalist. Picasso's friend first, he was soon to become Stein's. She took to his humor, his pithy comments, his tales—even his restlessness. "Nobody but Guillaume," she wrote, "it was the Italian in Guillaume... could make fun of his hosts, make fun of their guests, make fun of their food and spur them on to always greater and greater effort."[47]

Stein was deeply impressed with the technical and syntactical innovations Apollinaire brought to poetry. In his volume of poems, *Alcools* (1913), he banished punctuation while highlighting the music of verse. He considered artificial standardized punctuation marks to be "useless" in bringing out the tones and rhythms inherent in the words themselves. Indeed, many of his verses in *Alcools* and his other works were set to music and sung by the finest musicians of his day and ours.

Exciting to Stein as well were Apollinaire's art criticisms. His essays on Picasso's Rose Period, on Matisse's Fauvism, and on Italian Futurism, for example, did much to make known the works of many an avant-garde painter. Although, when published as a collection entitled *Les Peintres cubistes* (1913), many an artist looked at them critically (Braque and Picasso considered his critiques "shallow"), all were grateful to him for having been one of the earliest exponents of cubism.

Meanwhile, Stein's full intellectual and creative existence was complemented by an increasing number of American visitors. Making new connections as well as renewing old ties was in some cases highly pleasurable—and rewarding. Friends such as Dr. Claribel and her sister, Etta Cone, whose habit it was to make long visits to Paris, also became great art collectors. The fifty-one-year-old New Englander, Mildred Aldrich, editor and critic for the *Boston Evening Transcript,* among other journals, moved to France, remaining there until her death in 1928. Most important of all was Alice B. Toklas's visit to Paris in 1907, for it was she who would become Stein's lifelong secretary, housekeeper, friend, and lover.

Toklas was a San Franciscan by birth. After her mother's death, when she was only in her teens, she ran the household for her father, a property owner of Polish origin and Jewish faith. Although well versed in the arts of cooking, gardening, and needlework, Alice was also a cultured person, enjoying theater, opera, and literature—and Henry James was one of her favorite writers, as he was Stein's. Unmarried at thirty, and with her father's unenthusiastic consent, she and a friend, Harriet Levy, decided to go to Paris. Having met Mr. and Mrs. Michael Stein on one of their return trips to San Francisco, Toklas had been inspired by their exciting description of the city of lights.

Shortly after Toklas and her friend arrived in Paris, they visited Michael and Sarah Stein in their flat on rue Madame and were duly impressed by the art work on their walls, especially Matisse's. Stein was present on that occasion and Toklas was immediately drawn to her. She had just returned from a summer in Italy, and in Toklas's words, looked like

a golden brown presence burned by the Tuscan sun and with a golden glint in her warm brown hair. She was dressed in a warm brown corduroy suit. She wore a large round coralbrooch and when she talked, very little, or laughed, a good deal, I thought her voice came from this brooch. It was unlike anyone else's voice—deep, full, velvety, like a great contralto's, like two voices.[48]

The interest Toklas manifested in Stein must have been reciprocated since she was invited to rue de Fleurus the following day.

Although Toklas had taken the precaution of sending her hostess a *petit bleu,* informing her that she would be about a half hour late for the rendezvous, when she finally arrived, Stein had become, she wrote, "a vengeful goddess and I was afraid."[49] Despite this ominous beginning, they then decided to take a walk in the Luxembourg Gardens. According to accounts, it was for both ladies, love at first sight.

Although Toklas still lived with Harriet Levy, she went to Stein's home daily. It was only a matter of time before she settled into a routine designed to please Stein in every way. Toklas attended to all the secretarial work, received guests or turned them away, depending upon the writer's mood of the moment, and took care of the household chores, particularly the planning of the meals, which was such an important part of life at 27, rue de Fleurus.

When it came to an appreciation or even an understanding of avant-garde art, Toklas, accustomed to the charm and ease of representational paintings, such as Millet's *Man with a Hoe,* had much to learn. When confronted with Picasso's *Portrait of Gertrude Stein* and *The Demoiselles from Avignon,* or other Picasso creations, Toklas was unnerved by the distortions and savage primitivism of the angular faces with their twisted noses, strange eyes, and masklike faces.

In time, however, under Stein's tutelage, Toklas understood that behind Picasso's forms and colors existed raw creative energy. The monumental *The Demoiselles from Avignon,* Stein wrote years later, was "a composition that had neither a beginning nor an end, a composition of which one corner was as important as another corner, in fact the composition of cubism."[50] Moreover, his work was in keeping with Einstein's vision of the phenomenological world. Picasso's concept of space, for example, as expanding in dimension so as to assimilate time, no longer obliged him to depict a continuous unbroken space to be observed from but a single point of view. Although acknowledging cubism's debt to Cézanne, Picasso, she emphasized, was the real prophet of his day.

It is true certainly in the water colors of Cézanne that there was a tendency to cut the sky not into cubes but into arbitrary divisions, there too had been the pointilism of Seurat and his followers, but that had

nothing to do with cubism, because all these other painters were preoccupied with their technique which was to express more and more what
they were seeing, the seduction of thing seen.[51]

Leo's view was diametrically opposed to Stein's. That he, a perceptive critic, castigated Picasso's latest works, condemning the
painter's use of "Negroid things," may have been motivated by
more than purely analytical reasons. He perhaps sensed that the
advent of *The Demoiselles from Avignon* marked the beginning
of the end of what had been an emotional and intellectual bond
between Picasso, Stein, and himself.

Points of contention between brother and sister increased. Not
only did they disagree concerning Picasso's newfound cubism, but
even more important was the fact that Stein was still wounded by
her brother's cool reception of *Three Lives*. That she was still trying to find a publisher for her short stories, as well as for *The
Making of Americans*, added to her distress. Yet, how could a
publisher take such a financial risk: a nearly one-thousand page
novel with endless discussions, flashbacks, and repetitions. Stein
was facing failure upon failure until one day, ironically enough,
May Bookstaver (now the married Mrs. Charles Knoblauch), who
had caused Stein so much grief, was finally the one to find a publisher for *Three Lives* (1909). Like Proust, Stein also had to pay
for the publication of her work. Unlike Proust, however, the director of the Grafton Press, commenting on her poor grammar,
suggested she use a competent editor to revise her manuscript.
Understandably, she rejected his advice.

As Stein grew increasingly distant from her brother, she became
more and more dependent upon Toklas for all her needs, including the typing of her manuscripts and the running of the house.
On the maid's day off, Toklas, whose goal was to please Stein,
cooked American food, which she knew Stein loved. When Stein
needed a listener for the reading of her work, Toklas was there,
always attentive, always adoring. When Stein felt like taking a
walk through Saint-Germain, the Luxembourg Gardens, along the
quays, or for windowshopping, she would accompany her.

As their love grew, Stein may have intended to celebrate her
newfound rapture with "Ada" (Alice). A cubistic love poem imbued with its own revolutionary grammatical and syntactical
forms, including the divestiture of verbal and clausal associations,

the composition secretes a highly emotional love experience. The burden of ferreting out any and all meaning in this ambiguous work is placed upon the reader. Paradoxically, "Ada" tells both a personal and depersonalized tale. Vague implications or clues placed here and there suggest a puzzlelike approach to writing.

In hermetic and guarded terms, "Ada" reveals a series of facts and events relating to Toklas's family and her relationships with her father, mother, and brother, but also—and in the most subtle of terms—her reticent or repressed approach to sex. Was Stein alluding to Toklas's possible frigidity? or simply to her inhibitions? Whatever the innuendoes, in "Ada" Stein conveyed her love for and need of Toklas: "Trembling was all living, living was all loving, some one was then the other one. Certainly this one was loving this Ada then. And certainly Ada all her living then was happier in living than any one else who ever could, who was, who is, who ever will be living."

As the days and months passed, Stein and Toklas seemed to feel more sexually and emotionally comfortable with one another. Indeed, they gave each other pet names: "Lovey" for Stein and "Pussy" for Toklas. In due course, a family structure came into being. Stein was the husband and Toklas, the wife. In time, however, and this, too is significant in understanding such a relationship, Stein became the "Baby" and Toklas, the caring, nurturing, and comforting "Mother."

Love, however, exacts a price. At times Toklas became possessive and jealous of Stein's past loves as well as of any man or woman to whom she felt Stein might be attracted. When, for example, she learned of Stein's former intimate relations with Etta Cone, she vented her spleen. Years later, in 1932, for the same reason, Toklas's rage assumed such proportions that she destroyed Stein's letters to May Bookstaver. Another incident occurred the following year. Stein happened to come across her manuscript of "Q.E.D." She gave it to Louis Bromfield to read. Although he liked it and considered it suitable for publication, Stein realized that to make such information public would cause Toklas great pain; accordingly, she gave the manuscript to her to do with it as she wished. The result: it was printed in 1950, after Stein's death.[52] Nor was Toklas one to forget or forgive what she considered to be a slight. Although she gave the impression of being passive and tender, she was all but that when she thought that her well-being or love-object was threatened. It must also be noted that she had a will of iron and was fearless in giving her opinion and reactions to the visitors at 27, rue de Fleurus.

Another case in point was Toklas's jealousy of what she believed to be Stein's interest in Mabel Dodge Luhan. An emancipated and wealthy hostess, four times married and with multiple lovers, Dodge was the friend of celebrities par excellence. (She established an artists' colony in Taos and invited D. H. Lawrence to live there.) Stein and Dodge had met in Paris. Impressed with her and her writings, the latter invited Stein and Toklas to visit her at Villa Curionia in Florence. Toklas must have noted Dodge's obvious delight in Stein's company, for she wrote in her *Intimate Memoirs,* that, at lunch one day, "Gertrude, sitting opposite me in Edwin's [Dodge's husband] chair, sent me such a strong look over the table that it seemed to cut across the air to me in a band of electrified steel—a smile traveling across on it—powerful—Heavens! I remember it so keenly!" Alice suddenly rose from her chair and walked out. Stein, concerned when she failed to return, followed her, then came back to inform Dodge that "She [Toklas] does not want to come to lunch. She feels the heat today."[53] Evidently, Stein could no longer even toy with the idea of straying—at least not with Mabel Dodge.

However, when Toklas liked Stein's friends—Picasso, for example—she helped them willingly if situations warranted collaboration. A case in point is the now-famous "Rousseau banquet," about which each participant narrated his or her own version. Organized in 1908 (the spring or fall, even the season is uncertain) to honor the aging, frail, and unsuccessful painter, Henri Rousseau (*Le Douanier*), the dinner took place in Picasso's Bateau Lavoir studio. Whether the banquet was initiated by Picasso, to commemorate his purchase of a Rousseau canvas for which he paid five francs (the picture dealer informed him he could always paint over the canvas and use it again); or whether it was Leo who had thought up the event when chatting one afternoon with Fernande Oliver at the Bateau Lavoir and Rousseau stopped by to rest after giving a violin lesson, is not known.

According to Stein, Apollinaire had been elected to bring Rousseau to the party after which the festivities would begin: banquet, poetry recitations, singing, and story telling. Such well-laid plans, however, were not to materialize. Seemingly, the painter Marie Laurencin, Apollinaire's great love, unaccustomed to drink, imbibed quite heavily, as did the others who were waiting for Rousseau. By the time the guest of honor arrived, she was so drunk that she began dancing, flinging her arms about in what she thought were exotic postures. Just as suddenly, Fernande broke the bad news: the caterer had failed to bring the food. Since it was Sunday, his shop was closed. What to do? She and Toklas rushed out to buy quantities of *riz à la Valenciennes*, which they then prepared and served to the guests: the Steins, Braque, Salmon, Laurencin, Raynal, and others. Rousseau's painting, draped in flags and wreaths, was hung, and the banquet began. Apollinaire quieted Laurencin's intermittent and seemingly uncontrollable cries at least long enough to deliver his spirited and moving homage, concluding with "Long live! Long live Rousseau!" Toasts followed. When it was Salmon's turn to address the guests, he got up on the already rickety table, said what he had to say, took hold of a glass of wine, drank it, and suddenly began to fight. Leo tried to protect the frail Rousseau and his violin from harm while the others seized Salmon and took him by force to the other room, after which he feel into a deep sleep. Songs and dances followed far into the night and Rousseau even performed on his violin.

Such spirited interludes did not diminish the tensions that seemed to be increasing at rue de Fleurus. The closer the Stein–Toklas relationship grew, the more strained became Stein's rapport with Leo and more misunderstandings, artistic and emotional, developed. When Toklas finally moved into the Stein household in 1910, Leo pretended to be pleased with her presence, he himself being involved in a love affair with Nina Auzias (a model he married in 1921). A profound and searing wound was festering, however: he who had been his sister's mentor and virtually exclusive companion, who had shaped her taste in art, had suddenly been displaced. Feelings of bitterness and rancor flaired, giving way to bouts of pettiness.

Stein, now queen at 27, rue de Fleurus ("slowly I was knowing that I was a genius and it was happening"[54]), had usurped Leo's kingly power. He who had played the role of surrogate father had now become a negative and destructive force in her life. Because his cold and hurtful assessments of her writings were not objective she saw them as a futile attempt to increase his waning dominance in their relationship. If she were to evolve intellectually, she reasoned, and fully enjoy the pleasures in her newfound love, only one road was open to her. She severed ties with her brother, thus ending their symbioltic relationship. Leo's hurt was profound, but she wrote, "It did not trouble me and as it did not trouble me, I knew it was not true and a little as it did not trouble me he knew it was not true. But it destroyed him for me and it destroyed me for him."[55]

Now that Leo could no longer regard himself as superior to his sister, he knew he would have to pursue *one* rather than multiple careers, and prove himself in a specific domain. He failed. A psychological inability to grow into manhood served to prolong his already overly long adolescence. He was a true *puer:* brilliant, talented, perceptive, charming, but never able to summon the energy or self-discipline necessary to stop veering from one interest to another.[56]

The matriarchate had now displaced the patriarchate. Stein was in her element. Her reaction to the break with her brother was verbalized in *Two: Gertrude Stein and Her Brother.* The ambiguous "Two" of the title, suggests a transference from her close relationship with her brother to her newfound love. The word *sound,* repeated throughout much of the volume in what is an unfortunately dull piece of writing, indicates the deafness existing between brother and sister: their inability to *hear,* to communicate, to understand each other:

The sound there is in them comes out from them. Each one of them has sound in them. Each one of them has sound coming out of them. There are two of them. One of them is a man and one of them is a woman. They are both living. They are both ones that quite enough are knowing.[57]

The change in the relationship between brother and sister after Toklas became a presence in the household, was slow, virtually imperceptible, and described in short but revealing sentences by Stein, the scientific observer: "She was changing. He was changing. They were not changing. Sound was coming out of them, that was coming out of them. Sound was coming out of each one of them. He was one. She was one. He was one."[58]

Resentment did not dissipate between brother and sister even after Leo's departure from 27, rue de Fleurus in 1913 and his move to Settignano. Financial matters had to be settled and the all-important division of the paintings had to be made. Although

problematic at first, Leo demonstrated a certain largesse in this
matter as the following letter suggests:

The Cézanne apples have a unique importance to me that nothing can
replace. The Picasso landscape is not important in any such sense. We
are, as it seems to me on the whole, both so well off now that we needn't
repine. The Cézannes had to be divided. I am willing to leave you the
Picasso oeuvre, as you left me the Renoir, and you can have everything
except that . . . and just as I was glad that Renoir was sufficiently indifferent to you so that you were ready to give them up, so I am glad that
Pablo is sufficiently indifferent to me that I am willing to let you have all
you want of it.[59]

Despite the contretemps with Leo, others emerged, namely with
Mabel Dodge, as previously mentioned. Interestingly, Stein's rela-
tionship proved to be fruitful in that it was during her visit in
Florence that she wrote "Portrait of Mabel Dodge at the Villa
Curionia." The brief literary portrait so delighted her hostess that
she had three hundred copies printed and bound.

Stein's portrait of Dodge is one of many texts of this genre that
make use of a highly personal mimetic verbal technique intended
to capture an individual's type. Less orthodox than Stein's portraits of Picasso, Matisse, and Cézanne, but still using the syntactical device of repetition, thereby calling up memory and
sensation as well as situation, Dodge's portrait begins expan-
sively, "The days are wonderful and the nights are wonderful and
the life is pleasant." Although ellipses, conjunctions, present participles are peppered throughout the text, as in previous portraits,
a greater degree of coherence is also evident. Stein, for example,
grasps at certain personal details (chair, blanket, vase, etc.) to
which she responds, rather than depicting the house or the land-
scaped grounds as a whole. Still, the ideas formulated are banal.
She intimates, for example, that no one can experience any event
or person fully: "There is not all of any visit." Less vigorous and
intense than her portraits of Picasso and Matisse, perhaps because
she was dealing with a less-noteworthy personality, the portrait of
Dodge, nevertheless, thrilled its subject. Upon her return to the
United States (1912), Dodge gave copies of the "Portrait" to those
who might be interested in reading something by the now-famous
hostess, Stein. Interest in the American exile was now high and
Dodge was asked and accepted to do an article on Stein's writ-

ings for the magazine *Arts and Decoration* (1913). This special
issue was focused exclusively on what was to become the landmark New York Armory Exhibition, which shocked so many of
its viewers and critics. Reviled by some and praised by the avant-
garde, the Armory Exhibition featured the works of Marcel
Duchamp—his notorious *Nude Descending the Staircase*—along
with canvases by Picasso, Braque, Matisse, Delaunay, some of
which came from the Stein collection. Dodge's perceptive article,
"Speculations, or Post-Impressionism in Prose," compared Stein's
verbal technique with Picasso's linear pictorial vision. She also
emphasized its rhythmical and musical qualities: "It is so exquis-
itely rhythmical and cadenced that if we read it aloud and receive
it as pure sound, it is like a kind of sensuous music."[60] Carl Van
Vechten, promotor and music critic, who was to become Stein's
longtime friend, also wrote an article, "How to Read Gertrude
Stein" (*Trend*, 1914), underscoring the multiple tonal qualities
implicit in her language. "Miss Stein . . . has really turned language into music, really made its sound more important than its
sense." Other articles followed.

Stein was more than delighted. She thought her literary future
assured. She was wrong. Although well-known in avant-garde circles in America and in Paris, mostly for her art collection and for
her salon, the road to publication would be rocky and arduous.
Trips to England to arrange for the printing of some of her writings, in addition to letters from friends urging such publication,
led, after multiple rejections, to the appearance of *Tender Buttons*
in 1914, but *Many Many Women* and *The Making of Americans*
still remained unpublished.

Stein was not one to remain glum. Rejection had become for
her a fact of life. She did not let the hurt she experienced detract
from the pleasure she enjoyed being the focus of attention for artists drawn to or living in Paris: Marsden Hartley, Max Weber,
Alfred Maurer, William Glackens, Arthur Dove, Joseph Stella,
Charles Demuth, Charles Sheeler, Picabia, and more. Thoughtful
in many ways, she arranged introductions for certain artists with
Picasso and Matisse, and immortalized some of the painters who
visited her—Hartley, for example, who was featured as a character—M–N H—in her play, *IIIIIIIIII*. Questions were posed not
only concerning the ambiguous text, but also the meaning of the
title: was it a narcissistic reference to the first person singular?
was it to be identified with the roman numeral?

When Stein suggested to Hartley that he ask Alfred Stieglitz to print her play, she became her own publicist. Photographer and editor of the magazine *Camera Work,* and promoter of avant-garde art in his gallery "291," Stieglitz had already published her portraits of Picasso and Matisse in his magazine (1912). Now that he was preparing for a Hartley show, she felt it would be a golden opportunity to print her play, *IIIIIIIII,* in the catalogue. He accepted, but printed only an extract.

Stein's fame was growing. The creator of the "abstract word portrait," as these were now called, and the author of *Three Lives* and *Tender Buttons,* her writings inspired a whole new iconographic and programmatized approach to the literary text. A combination of cubist vision, the mechanistic age, and a Dadaistic disregard for logical syntactical sequences and traditional grammatical devices, her verbal pyrotechnics were uniquely Steinian. Indeed, the "new symbolic-associative language" that emerged in her writings, known as *Steinese,* began to be practiced in the pictorial domain by Hartley, Dove, Demuth, and the flamboyant Picabia whose paintings *Dances at the Spring* and *Procession* had already made tongues wag.

Having cast aside older artists, particularly Matisse with his "decorative" canvases, Stein was forever befriending new ones.[61] Another Spanish painter who had made his way to Paris in 1905, Juan Gris (1887–1927), had also made his home in a studio in the Bateau Lavoir and was instrumental, together with Picasso and Braque, in developing cubism, especially in its evolution from analytic to synthetic. Gris's non-figurative paintings and collages in generally muted colors and severe and restrained lines did not win the recognition he sought. Taken by Gris's still lifes and collages, Stein purchased among others, his *Roses, Glass and Bottle,* and *Book and Glasses.* It was only a matter of time until she became his champion, allegedly helping him out financially when his situation became desperate.

It was 1914. The politics and boundaries of Europe were about to shift. Signs of war were becoming increasingly evident. Apolitical and a wishful thinker, Stein failed to take seriously such events as the assassination of the Archduke Ferdinand at Sarajevo. Making light of the happening, she and Toklas left for London (July 6, 1914) as planned. Although their cross-channel

venture was rewarding for Stein (she signed the desired contract for the English edition of *Three Lives*), it also saw the outbreak of World War I.

Unable to return to Paris, Stein and Toklas spent anxious days wondering about the fate of their friends caught in Paris and the safety of the manuscripts and paintings left in the unprotected apartment. Their lives in London, however, were far from dismal. Stein met and had long discussions with intellectually stimulating people, and especially Alfred North Whitehead, the mathematician and philosopher whom Stein alluded to as a *genius*. His creation of a new vocabulary and a new system of universal ideas had enabled Whitehead to rectify what he deemed to be the faulty traditional categories of philosophy and their inability to convey the essential interrelation of matter, space, and time. With regard to religion, Whitehead had rejected the belief in a perfect and omnipotent Deity, suggesting instead that God was interdependent with the world and developed with it.

Despite her active intellectual and social life, Stein was eager to return home. No sooner had the Germans been turned back at the Marne than a sense of joy and release so overwhelmed Stein and Toklas that they wept. They made plans to return to Paris. Such a venture in time of war was no simple task. Nevertheless, on October 17, thanks to a military pass that Mrs. Alfred North Whitehead had secured for them, Stein and Toklas were given permission to return to France.

The difficulties that beset them in a Paris deprived of fuel and food encouraged these great "patriots" to find warmer and more hospitable climes. They journeyed to Spain where they remained nearly a year, staying a good part of the time on the beautiful and serene island of Majorca. Because funds were low, Stein decided to sell to her brother Michael her last remaining Matisse—the famous *Femme au Chapeau*—for four thousand dollars. It was during this pleasurable period that Stein took to reading biographies and autobiographies. Not only did she find this literary genre a source of entertainment and an enriching experience, inviting views of new landscapes and different forms and styles, but the intimate dialogues inherent to biographies and autobiographies enabled her to enter the psyches of the characters portrayed. Perhaps Stein was already musing about a fresh approach to biography—the kind she might one day write.

The time spent in Spain allowed Stein to complete "Farragut; or, A Husband's Recompense," a transcription in poetic prose of her discussions, disagreements, and incompatibilities with Toklas. Their daily relationship as husband and wife, although disclosing an ever-evolving and deepening love, also verbalized, in Stein's coded confessional tone, their quarrels and humorous interludes. Nor is there a dearth of eroticism in her Majorcan works. In "I Have No Title to Be Successful," she notes, "For instance our loving. We are loving. We can say that honestly." In "The King or Something," Stein remarks: "Lift brown eggs / To me." And "Lifting Belly" encourages her to comment on their "heterosexual" relationship. "Darling wifie is so good," and "Little hubbie is good." "Please be the man" followed by "I am the man." Nor are comments on her partner's pleasing features lacking: "Pussy how pretty you are," or graphic sequences, revealing the "stretches and stretches of happiness" her lover gives her, "Lifting belly is so strong. I love cherish idolise adore and worship you." "Lifting belly high / That is what I adore always more and more." "I can go on with lifting belly forever." Toklas's ability to yield her infinite sexual delights is expressed in the following:

> Kiss my lips. She did.
> Kiss my lips again she did.
> Kiss my lips over and over and over again she did.[62]

Returning to Paris on June 20, 1916, the pair decided to help the war effort. To this end, Stein learned to drive and began working for the American Fund for French Wounded. The pair's job, which involved classifying supplies sent to the various hospitals in France and giving out blankets and clothes to refugees, took the two to such places as Perpignan, Nîmes, Mulhouse. Their efforts made them the proud recipients of the Médaille de la Reconnaissance Française.

The war was over. Apollinaire, who had suffered such a severe head wound during the fighting that it required a trepanning, was left in such weakened condition that he succumbed to influenza during the epidemic of 1918. Matisse had moved to Nice. Leo, who had spent the war years in America undergoing psychoanalysis and writing articles in a desultory manner on art, moved back to Settignano in 1919. Although he had written his sister several letters, she never responded. She was determined to cut

ties completely. (They met only once again, in 1931, at the Place Saint-Germain-des-Prés. Stein bowed to her brother, but uttered not a word, and that very evening, she wrote "She Bowed to Her Brother.")

Friends, acquaintances, and enemies continued to make their way to rue de Fleurus. Sylvia Beach, the founder of Shakespeare and Company, a library service for American and English writers, brought Sherwood Anderson to visit at 27, rue de Fleurus on June 13, 1921. The author of the best-seller *Winesburg, Ohio,* Anderson heard all sorts of stories about this American in Paris: comments on her loud laugh, her languid nature, which kept her reclining on a couch for hours on end, her disconcerting habit of staring at newcomers "with strange cold eyes."[63] He was particularly intrigued by the manner in which Stein combined and fashioned words, giving old ones a fresh flavor and aroma and new ones a distinct tinge of the old manner. What most impressed Anderson was *Tender Buttons.* A catalyst for him, Stein's verbal prowess and linguistic insight had gone a long way in expanding his vision. Her manner of manipulating tenses, verbs, and sentences intrigued him: "I am working fairly steadily on the sentence," she wrote years later. "I am making a desperate effort to find out what is and isn't a sentence."[64]

Friendship between the two grew. When Stein decided to publish a collection of experimental portraits and theater pieces, *Geography and Plays,* at her own expense, she asked Anderson to write the introduction because "you are really the only person who really knows what it is all about." He agreed and summed up his debt and reactions to this miraculous "worker of words":

For me the work of Gertrude Stein consists in a rebuilding, an entirely new recasting of life, in the city of words. Here is one artist who has been able to accept ridicule, who has even forgone the privilege of writing the great American novel, uplifting our English speaking stage, and wearing the bays of the great poets, to go live among the little housekeeping words, the swaggering bullying street-corner words, the honest working, money saving words, and all the other forgotten and neglected citizens of the sacred and half forgotten city.[65]

Stein, the "restorer of words," had bewitched Anderson, and she was deeply appreciative of his praise: "I am awfully touched by what you say of me but you know that your feeling about my work is more precious to me than that of any one else."[66]

When Anderson introduced Ernest Hemingway to Stein in 1921, he, too, was taken with this American in exile. He described her as "very big but not tall and was heavily built like a peasant woman. She had beautiful eyes and a strong German-Jewish face ... [a] mobile face and ... lovely, thick, alive immigrant hair." So powerful was her "personality that when she wished to win anyone over to her side she would not be resisted."[67] Strangely enough, Hemingway was physically attracted to this monolith Stein. Years later, he confessed to having wanted "to fuck her and she knew it and it was a good healthy feeling and made more sense than some of the talk."[68]

Toklas reacted differently to Hemingway. Strong and increasingly dogmatic, according to Hemingway, she was jealous of any intruder who might threaten her relationship with her beloved. Perhaps she sensed Stein's physical attraction for the young and handsome Hemingway. Her dislike for the man was overt from the very start, and Hemingway's aversion to this "hairy-lipped" emaciated steely woman, who reminded him of "a little piece of electric wire," was reciprocal. Toklas's jealousy, he was convinced, was to blame for many of Stein's severed relationships. Early in his friendship with Stein, the perceptive young Hemingway understood Toklas's "cruel erotic demands were much to Stein's taste. . . . In exchange she acted as Stein's willing secretary and social slave."[69] Nor was Stein less autocratic and demanding in her relationships: as long as Hemingway remained docile, a good listener and learner, an admirer of her paintings and writings, all went well. Stein was his mentor at this period: she was the one who suggested he leave journalism and focus his energy on creative writing, who explained how he should use rhythm and repetition in his writing and how he could learn to *concentrate*. It was she as well who spoke to him excitedly about bullfights and the matador Joselito, encouraging him to visit Spain.[70]

Although she liked his "Kiplingesque" poetry, she was critical of his short story, "Up in Michigan," perhaps because it included a detailed sexual scene, thus making it *inaccrochable,* comparing it to a painting that could not be exhibited because of its prurience.[71] Her prudishness, which she denied, surprised Hemingway. In time, there developed a free-flowing quality between them. The two spoke on any and all subjects—even homosexuality—about which she was convinced he knew nothing. She would educate him in this domain, she thought, in "the mechanics of it," why the act did not disgust those who performed it (she was at this time against male homosexuality but changed later) and why it was not degrading to either participant." Stein maintained:

The main thing is that the act male homosexuals commit is ugly and repugnant and afterwards they are disgusted with themselves. They drink and take drugs, to palliate this, but they are disgusted with the act and they are always changing partners and cannot be really happy. . . . In women, it is the opposite. They do nothing that they are disgusted by and nothing that is repulsive and afterwards they are happy and they can lead happy lives together.[72]

Her insights on homosexuality, Hemingway remarked, enabled him to write "A Sea Change," a short story focusing on lesbianism. But Hemingway excited Stein and she thrived on his presence. He, too, benefited from her knowledge and even used her now-famous statement, "You are all a lost generation," in *The Sun Also Rises* (1926). He showed his appreciation by doing the impossible: as assistant editor of the *Transatlantic Review*, he saw to the publication of nine installments of *The Making of Americans*.

A break between the two was bound to occur however; Hemingway was not the type to remain a disciple for long. Nor did he believe, as did Stein, that "Twentieth century literature *is* Gertrude Stein." She resented any writer whom she thought might someday surpass her. "If you brought up Joyce twice, you would not be invited back. . . . I cannot remember Gertrude Stein ever speaking well of any writer who had not written favorably about her work or done something to advance her career."[73]

The rift came with the publication of Hemingway's *A Farewell to Arms* (1929). Not really a severing of relationships, it was more of a dismissal. "She had, or Alice had, a sort of necessity to break off friendships and she only gave real loyalty to people who were inferior to her. She had to attack me because she learned to write dialogue from me just as I learned the wonderful rhythms in prose from her."[74]

There are varying accounts of the split between Stein and Hemingway. Toklas seemingly informed Hadley, Hemingway's wife, who frequently stopped by at rue de Fleurus, that Stein was busy and could see no one. Hemingway's account in *A Moveable Feast* is different. He had been invited to Stein's home and after the maid greeted him and poured him some eau-de-vie, he waited. Suddenly, he heard a most sordid argument between Stein and Toklas.

I heard someone speaking to Miss Stein as I had never heard one person speak to another; never, anywhere, ever. Then Miss Stein's voice came pleading and begging, saying, "Don't, pussy. Don't. Don't, please, don't. I'll do anything, pussy, but please don't do it. Please don't. Please don't, pussy."[75]

Stein's explanation of their rift in *The Autobiography of Alice B. Toklas* was rife with disdain. She referred to Hemingway, who prided himself on his manliness and courage, as "yellow"; as a writer "who does it without understanding it, in other words who takes training." Although Toklas, Hemingway commented, had warned Stein not to invite him to the house any more, she countered her interdict by welcoming him, then verbally stabbing him through the heart when labeling him a cosmopolitan writer: "Hemingway, after all you are ninety percent Rotarian." "Can't you make it eighty percent?" he asked. "No," Stein replied. "I can't." Yet, when Hemingway returned to Paris in 1944 and happened upon Stein, he told her that he had "always loved her and she said she loved me too which was, I think, the truth from both of us." In a letter to Edmund Wilson, Hemingway remarked that "Alice had the ambition of the devil" and that her jealousy was to blame for their break: "Alice was her evil angel as well as her great friend." So profound was Hemingway's rage toward Toklas that he refused to allow his correspondence with Stein to be published during the lifetime of this infamous woman.[76]

Other notables also made their way to 27, rue de Fleurus: F. Scott Fitzgerald, at the pinnacle of his fame with a backlog of *This Side of Paradise* (1920) and *The Great Gatsby* (1926); and Janet Flanner, who signed her articles for *The New Yorker* as Genet, and who, although not always in admiration of Stein's writings, remained her friend. Artists were always plentiful in Stein's entourage. Jacques Lipchitz, who made a bust of Stein, endowed her with a Buddha-like countenance. Jo Davidson's portrait-sculpture of Stein transformed her into an Egyptian scribe. Davidson introduced Stein to Jean Cocteau, who told her that one of her lines had inspired him to write his strange work, *The Potomak*. Man Ray, the surrealist photographer, immortalized Stein with his camera.

T. S. Eliot was not favorably disposed to Stein's literary style. When visiting at 27, rue de Fleurus with Lady Rothermere, he asked to know the name of the mentor who had advised her to use so many split infinitives. "Henry James," she retorted. At the opposite pole was Stein's meeting with Edith Sitwell. Fascinated by language and eccentric in her own abstract approach to words, Sitwell admired Stein's pieces. Albeit she warned young authors not to take Stein as a model, she considered her work "valuable because of its revivifying qualities" and its "considerable beauty." Virginia and Leonard Woolf, whom Stein approached in the hope that their Hogarth Press would publish an English edition of *The Making of Americans,* were unfavorably disposed. Stein's enemies found her work overly hermetic, repetitive, and dull, even while a whole new generation of writers searching for fresh ways of expressing their feelings and ideas admired her language and style.

Stein felt she needed greater exposure, more readers, more listeners. Yet, when initially invited to lecture at Cambridge and Oxford, she did not accept. Her reasons? Her fear of appearing in public, of confronting so many people alone onstage. After the acute phase of her panic subsided, she finally agreed (1925).

Her decision taken, she realized there were concrete ways of assuaging her terror: she would write out her lecture, "Composition as Explanation," and simply read it. One of the themes with which she would deal was that of the "outlaw," the one possessed of a revolutionary spirit in the arts or in other disciplines, who is made to feel like a virtual pariah by traditional society. "Those who are creating the modern composition authentically are naturally only of importance when they are dead because by that time the modern composition having become past is classified and the description of it is classical." She also explored her ideas on style and syntax, her rejection of conventional modes of expression, concretizing these as she traced her own literary development from "Melanctha" to *The Making of Americans.* In her struggle to divest herself of the popular chronological narrative, she created the "prolonged present," then the "continuous present," thus eliminating the antiquated notions of a beginning, middle, and end in fictional writings.

Not everyone in the audience was receptive to Stein's insights and her repetitive and discursive style. Nevertheless, her listeners —enthusiasts and hecklers—were responsive. Little did the less favorably disposed realize Stein's indomitable force when they attempted to lead her into blunder on details. Her straight-forwardness, her irony and humor enabled her to win round upon round.

Back in Paris and greatly relieved now that her speaking ordeal was over, Stein had the good fortune to meet the Missouri-born Virgil Thomson. He would be responsible for her branch-ing out into a whole new field: opera. That she should have suddenly taken to music, which she had never really liked and about which she knew little save for the operas she had attended when a student at Radcliffe, may be attributed to Thomson's passionate involvement in both this art form and in Stein's work in particular.

Thomson's piano score and vocal setting for an early Stein poem/portrait, "Susie Asado" (1926), marked the debut of a fruitful relationship between writer and composer. When he in-vited Stein to write a libretto for an opera, she accepted. He was not very pleased, however, with the theme she proposed; which revolved around American history and George Washington. After discussing the matter, Thomson wrote "we gave up history and chose saints, sharing a certain reserve toward medieval ones and Italian ones on the grounds that both had been overdone in the last century. Eventually our saints turned out to be Baroque and Spanish."[77] Although Stein had begun work on the libretto of *Four Saints in Three Acts* in the spring of 1927, the opera with its all-black cast, was produced, for lack of funding, only in 1934. It was a success.

The twenty-six-year-old Thomson, now one of Stein's inti-mates, introduced her to some of his young friends (Georges Hug-net, René Crevel, Christian Bérard, Pavel Tchelitchew, and others). Hugnet, whose father had financed his son's publishing business, brought out selections of *The Making of Americans* (1929) and *Ten Portraits* (1930), which he and Hugnet translated. Although Stein had no great love for the surrealists, whose work she considered facile and adolescent, she did admire Crevel's *Di-derot's Clavecin* for its "brilliant violence." Although modestly impressed with Tchelitchew's paintings, she held the highest opin-ion of Bérard's talents. Her friendships with this younger genera-tion of artists lasted as long as they were poor and unaccepted by the public. When, by 1932, Tchelitchew and Bérard had em-barked on their successful stage-set designing and painting ca-reers, earning praise from directors and critics alike, Stein's increasing envy of their popularity caused friction between them. Hugnet, too, was summarily dismissed from her entourage for not having printed Stein's name in large type as translator of his work *Enfances,* and his own, as author, in small letters. Stein's pettiness in such matters, her uncontrollable jealousy of the success of others at a time when the bulk of her work remained unpublished, created impossible tensions. If, for example, one of her protégés did not pay her the homage she felt was due her or did not sufficiently flatter her ego, or became well known and appreciated by the reading public, her ire was instantaneous. Without warning or explanation, the protégé would be barred from her home—heartlessly and abruptly. Resentment and bitterness had made increasing inroads in Stein's personality.

Times were changing and old friends disappearing. Juan Gris's death (1927) from asthma and uremic poisoning inspired her elegy, "The Life of Juan Gris. The Life and Death of Juan Gris," which she considered "the most moving thing" she had written.[78] Throughout Gris's career, Stein had remained one of his fervent admirers and had purchased some of his finest works: *The Table in Front of the Window, The Seated Woman, The Green Cloth.* Because few really appreciated his talents, according to Stein, to further his reputation she drew attention to his canvases in her essays. Stein's friendship with Gris was not, however, always smooth. Even here, personality problems led to intermittent spats and reconciliations.

Stein and Toklas had been spending their summers since 1924 in eastern France, not far from Lake Geneva. They had grown to love the landscape: its broad valleys, hills, and rivers, its variety of soft and harsh, even irregularly lined plains, its colorations, textures, and tonal qualities. She felt exhilarated, excited, and inspired by the extensive farmlands with their open spaces. She felt she could breathe here, away from the clutter of Paris.

So enamored of the region was Stein that she rented in 1929 a large seventeenth-century house on a hilltop in Bilignin, a few miles from Belley, the town in which the famous gastronome, Jean-Anthelme Brillat-Savarin, had been born. Her living space consisted of a courtyard, outbuildings, a terrace, and a garden. Here she gained the privacy she needed to write and the gardening facilities for which Toklas had longed. The berry plants and fruit trees surrounding the house allowed Toklas to make the pre-

serves that would adorn the breakfast tray she brought to Stein
daily and the liqueurs she would serve her after dinner. It was
also at this time that Stein acquired a French poodle puppy that
she named Basket.

Although her summers were spent far from Paris, visitors were
many: Picasso, his wife, Olga, their son, Paulot; Henry Luce, the
publisher of *Life* and *Time,* and his wife, Clare Boothe Luce; Cecil Beaton, the set designer; Bernard Fay, the historian; Carl Van
Vechten; Thornton Wilder; and Virgil Thomson. When there
were no guests, Stein had the time to write; the extensive space
and beguiling topography of the countryside inspired her to meditate. Her writings of this period took into account nature's pas-
toral tones and rhythms, accentuated by the variety of winds
soaring through the neighboring mountains and valleys, and the
variations in tonal qualities of the waterfall in the region.

Fascinated, if not obsessed with language, she yielded to her
bent in such theoretical compositions as "Saving the Sentence,"
"Arthur a Grammar," "Regular Regularly in Narrative," "A Vocabulary of Thinking"—all of which were included in her book,
How to Write (1931). A veritable initiation into the hermetic nature of language, this highly original work explores the various
emotional levels aroused by a sentence, a paragraph, and grammar in general.

To be cryptic and ambiguous satisfied Stein's élan. It did not
answer a publisher's dream. Rejection followed upon rejection. So
painful did she find her situation that she decided to finance her
own edition of her works, to be called the "Plain Edition," by
selling one of her early Picasso works, *Woman with a Fan* (1905).
Toklas was to be the manager of the publishing venture that
would include such works as *Lucy Church Amiably, How to
Write, Operas and Plays, Matisse Picasso and Gertrude Stein.*

Incredible as it may seem, Stein's efforts as publisher of her
own works were to come to a halt with *The Autobiography of
Alice B. Toklas* (1933)—a best-seller. The subject—her early
years in Paris—fascinated readers. Stein had a great deal to say
about both the world of the artists and writers who had visited
her home, and her art collection. She captivated her readers because of the liveliness and excitement she injected into the whole
era. Indeed, she resurrected it. She also appealed to the avant-
garde writer because of her style—her dislocation of traditional
narrative structure with her use of repetition and run-on sen-

tences. Perhaps most innovative was the fact that her autobiography was written from Toklas's point of view and in her words and speech patterns—not Stein's. Such an approach gave Stein greater detachment and freedom to speak scathingly about her enemies and more abandon in referring to her own "genius."

Although *The Autobiography* was a revisiting of Stein's past, in no way was it intended to be a history of her life. On the contrary, she considered it a fictional work able to advertise her worth and justify her theories concerning art and literature. Stein succeeded in her goal. Not only did Harcourt, Brace accept it immediately, but what gave Stein almost equal pleasure was the fact that an abridged version of *The Autobiography* was published in the *Atlantic Monthly*. The revenues nearly filled her empty coffers.

There were those, however, who derogated *The Autobiography*, contending that it was filled with factual errors, malicious statements, gossip, superficial tidbits, and chitchat. Leo attacked it, calling his sister a "liar." The editors of *transition*, Eugene and Marie Jolas, printed *Testimony against Gertrude Stein*, inviting Matisse, Braque, Tristan, Tzara, and others, to rectify the erroneous and disparaging statements made concerning them and their work. Matisse considered Mrs. Michael Stein "the really intelligently sensitive member of the family," though he did admire Leo. Braque commented, "Miss Stein obviously saw everything from the outside and never the real struggle we were engaged in. For one who poses as an authority of the epoch it is safe to say that she never went beyond the stage of the tourist."[79] Hemingway would bide his time before delivering his frontal attack.

An able promoter of Stein's *Autobiography* was Bernard Fay, the very Catholic and very reactionary historian, who was well placed in the highest circles. Indeed, he translated *The Autobiography* into French as did the novelist, Cesare Pavese, into Italian. The tide had turned: publishers now approached Stein. Not only would she be assured of the printing of many of her heretofore unpublished works, but of her future ones as well.

Coincidentally, the following year (1934) saw the spectacular production of *Four Saints in Three Acts*. Its all-black cast, in flagrant opposition to the Spanish characters; its cellophane scenery; its choreography and direction by Frederick Ashton and John Houseman; its orchestra conducted by Alexander Smallens—all contributed to earning it over sixty performances.

The time was ripe. Thirty years had elapsed since Stein had left her native land. Anderson and van Vechten suggested that she come to the United States to be feted. Although excited by the idea, the old problem of her anxiety once again returned. Her fears diminished at the thought of the financial soundness of such a venture. To speak at universities and clubs would not only promote the sales of her books, but would also assure the spreading of her fame.

Stein and Toklas arrived in New York City on October 24, 1934. Interviews, questions, articles, receptions awaited her upon her arrival in the United States for what was to be a triumphant tour. Whenever questioned by journalists, Stein was forthright. She had always been open and without reserve, committing herself, sometimes astutely and other times not, on many subjects. Prior to her departure, for example, she had been asked by the editors of *transition* why she chose to live abroad: "the United States is a country the right age to be born in and the wrong age to live in . . . a rich and well-nourished home but not a place to work . . . the most important country in the world—but a parent's home is never the place to work in."[80]

Stein had learned from her English experience to plan her lectures very carefully. She also decided to restrict the number of spectators to five hundred. Her first lecture, sponsored by the Museum of Modern Art ("Pictures") was given at the Colony Club in New York City; others were delivered at Columbia University ("The Gradual Making of *The Making of Americans*"), the University of Chicago ("Poetry and Grammar"), the Choate School ("How Writing Is Written"), Mt. Holyoke ("Plays"), Princeton, Bryn Mawr, the New School for Social Research, Amherst College, Harvard, Radcliffe, the University of Virginia, Tulane University, the Brooklyn Academy of Music, the Baltimore Museum, and other academic institutions, as well as in clubs and theaters throughout the United States. Although only Eleanor Roosevelt and not the president was able to attend the tea at the White House to which Stein had been invited, the occasion was memorable.

The outcome of Stein's tour in the United States was a virtual apotheosis. Exhausted and drained, she was nevertheless tremendously exhilarated. The top intellectuals had attended the lectures of the most famous American exile. Her ideas, dress, and thoughts were quoted in detail in newspapers and magazines all over the country. She made recordings and was asked to write articles or report on "American Education and Colleges," "American Newspapers," "American Crimes and How They Matter," "American States and Cities and How They Differ from Each Other," "American Food and American Houses." When it came time to depart, on May 12, 1935, Stein was almost sorry to leave her native land.

Good fortune also smiled in the publishing field. Random House agreed to bring out one of her books a year. Stein was delighted at the prospect of taking advantage of this offer with a difficult theoretical work: *The Geographical History of America; or, The Relation of Human Nature to the Human Mind.*

She chose to publish *The Geographical History of America* for personal reasons: it helped her probe certain problems that had arisen following the unexpected success of *The Autobiography of Alice B. Toklas* after so many years of failure. To be widely lauded disoriented Stein, who had built up a protective barrier against hurt. Old uncertainties returned to plague her and she was again faced with an identity crisis. A meditation on her quest for identity and the relationship of geography to the human personality, as stated in *The Geographical History of America,* formulates the steps to be taken in understanding the problems involved. Is one's identity built up slowly and painstakingly from within and independently of others? Or does it come into being through the reactions, observations, and opinions of others toward oneself? Responding to these queries, Stein uttered what has now become her celebrated Steinian phrase—"I am I because my little dog knows me."

In *The Geographical History of America,* Stein began in a relatively simple manner to explain that one must not be the person others consider oneself to be. One must simply evolve in terms of one's own self-image; thus can one be the person one is. When it came to analyze the identity of the artist, Stein's ideas were not only complex but ambiguous. She divided the human personality into two parts: Human Nature and the Human Mind. The former category is a concept that binds the creative spirit to the routine of life, to others, to memory of its own past, to biography, and thus intimately links it to the empirical world. The true genius—and she considered herself to be one—must seek higher spheres, transcending everyday reality while also reaching that purer and transpersonal state that is that of the Human Mind.

Thornton Wilder, who was called upon to write the preface to *The Geographical History of America,* although enthusiastic about the prospect, spent long hours listening to Stein explain her abstract, circuitous, and cryptic language.

Other books, such as *Everybody's Autobiography,* followed in the Random House publication schedule. Unlike *The Autobiography of Alice B. Toklas,* Stein's latest meditation upon her past dealt with far less interesting material: her American tour and the everyday people she met, her daily life at Bilignin, and family relationships. Humorous and informative at times, the monologues, long-winded passages, chatty, run-on sentences, repetitions, tendentious and tedious details do little to enhance the work. Nor did such self-serving statements as the following help enhance her image: "Einstein was the creative philosophic mind of the century and I have been the creative literary mind of the century." The critic for the *New York Times* expressed his dismay in no uncertain terms: "Easy to read and easy to forget, it is now obvious that Miss Stein's chief asset in writing is her colossal egotism and her chief inability to create character." He also commented on the "extraordinarily limited" nature of her mind.[81] Gone was the zest that had kindled the excitement injected into *The Autobiography of Alice B. Toklas;* gone as well was the fervor generated by one of the most creative periods in the arts.

Stein, at whom so much negative criticism had been aimed throughout her writing career, had virtually become inured to it. By now, she had many admirers and invitations to lecture in both England and the United States. Nor did her productivity as a writer diminish: *Listen to Me* appeared in 1936; and *Doctor Faustus Lights the Lights* in 1938; and a long essay on Picasso in 1938.

Other more routine matters, however, preoccupied her. She was obliged to give up her quarters at 27, rue de Fleurus. Early in 1938, Stein and Toklas moved to 15, rue Christine, which although relatively undistinguished had been made famous by Apollinaire in his "Lundi rue de Christine."

Armies were once again on the move in Europe in 1938, and although Stein considered herself politically uninvolved and detached, she had made some statements that were not only shockingly naïve, but also in utterly bad taste. When interviewed by Lansing Warren of the *New York Times Magazine* in 1934, for example, she suggested that Hitler be awarded the Nobel Peace

Prize. Using her so-called humor and circuitous powers of reason, she remarked that: "By driving out the Jews and the democratic and Left elements, he is driving out everything that conduces to activity. That means peace."[82] Was her thinking on political issues colored by the ideas of her very close friend and future German collaborator, Bernard Fay? Was he the one who urged her to prognosticate? to mimic the pacifist credo that there would *certainly* not be another European war?

During the late thirties, family and friends had tried to persuade Stein and Toklas to return to the United States, but to no avail. Stein could not be convinced that war was imminent. Nor did she believe that the situation in the Balkans, the fall of Austria, the Munich Pact, or Hitler's invasion of Poland, were portentous. Even Cecil Beaton, who visited Stein and Toklas in Bilignin, found her inability or unwillingness to face the political situation rather frightening. When war was finally declared, she was still underplaying its consequences.

Knowing the *right* people enabled Stein and Toklas, who were at Bilignin, to get a laissez-passer to go to Paris, to see to the safety of the paintings, and bring back winter clothes and various papers. Stein accomplished her mission and returned to Bilignin with Cézanne's *Portrait of Madame Cézanne* and Picasso's portrait of her. Since no funds were coming from the United States, she sold the Madame Cézanne portrait to a Swiss art dealer in 1943, thus assuring the couple's survival during the war.[83]

Warned once again to leave France, Stein and Toklas traveled to the American Consulate in Lyons, but seeing the long line of people intent upon going to the United States, they decided to remain at Bilignin. After all, she reasoned, it was just another "phony" war. The hardships created by the war did not seem to disrupt the smooth running of the home; perhaps there was a little less food and heat. Yes, there was one great inconvenience: the owner of the house Stein was renting at Bilignin wanted to return, forcing her and Toklas to move into a more modest home not far off, at Culoz. It took the detonation of bombs that began to fall near the rail center only a few miles from Bilignin, and the fact that young men in the village were dying, to make her believe in the reality of the war. In no way did Stein or Toklas help the war effort. Time was spent writing, walking, sawing wood, and cutting box hedges, which Stein found "soothing." She wrote children's stories, *To Do: A Book of Alphabets and Birthdays*.

There were, nevertheless, moments of terror. After Italy entered the war, she wrote in "The Winner Loses," published in *The Atlantic Monthly* (1940): "I was scared, completely scared, and my stomach felt very weak, because—well here we were right in everybody's path; any enemy that wanted to go any where might easily come here."[84] Stein decided it was time for them to leave. The American Consul would "fix up" their passports. No sooner had she made her decision than she wondered where they should go: Bordeaux, Spain, or Switzerland? When friends in the region assured them not only of their safety, but also of the many farms in the region, virtually guaranteeing them a plentiful food supply of eggs, meat, vegetables, and other aliments, they decided to stay.

They grow the things to eat right where you are, so there is no privation, as taking it away is difficult, particularly in the mountain, so there was plenty of meat and potatoes and bread and honey and we had some sugar and we even had all the oranges and lemons we needed and dates; a little short of gasoline for the car, but we learned to do what we wanted with that little, so we settled down to a comfortable and pleasantly exciting winter.[85]

Stein's physical well-being was always uppermost in her mind: "it would be awfully uncomfortable and I am fussy about my food. Let's not leave."[86]

Shockingly impervious to the sufferings of others during these war years, Stein and Toklas made it their practice not to listen to news reports on the radio, but rather to rely almost exclusively on a book of prophecy, *The Last Year of War* by Leonard Blake, for information concerning things to come. The prognostications of the innumerable saints of the region and elsewhere had not only predicted no war, but stated categorically, that if one were to break out, hostilities would cease within days. That Stein and Toklas had utmost faith in these pronouncements is almost inconceivable. Toklas did: Had not one of the saints declared that France would be betrayed by a non-French Catholic king? The verity of this prognostication had been proven in both in Belgium and in Italy. Stein seemed to go along with Toklas in these matters, but on some level must have had a good laugh. It also served to prevent her from thinking about the Holocaust and the suffering it brought in its wake.

Stein and Toklas remained at Bilignin throughout the war and the occupation. Neither encountered any difficulties despite the presence of the German Army. Indeed, Stein was pleased because the German soldiers admired her dog, and "were polite and considerate; they were, as the French said, correct."[87] Incredibly, no mention was made in her writings concerning the slaughter of millions by the Nazis in the concentration camps and elsewhere. Nor had Stein's knowledge of politics, always wanting, changed during the course of the war years. She trusted and had faith in Marshal Pétain and the Vichy government. Was her inability to see clearly into the political situation due in part to her fundamental egotism and self-centeredness? Was she considering her own welfare first and foremost and was she uninterested in that of the rest of the world? "Pétain was right to stay in France and he was right to make the armistice," she wrote, "and little by little I understood it. I always thought he was right to make the armistice, in the first place it was more comfortable for us who were here." Or was it her naïveté that encouraged her to believe that Pétain's armistice "was an important element in the ultimate defeat of the Germans," and to undertake a translation of the marshal's speeches, *Paroles aux Français, Messages et écrits (1934–1941)*. There is little doubt that Bernard Fay, the newly appointed director of the Bibliothèque Nationale under the Vichy government, and Stein's longtime friend, was instrumental in forming her regretfully shallow views.

In *Wars I Have Seen* (1945), Stein concentrates on the situation at Bilignin in greater detail, and, interestingly enough, uses few if any repetitions, run-on sentences, or puns. Although making mention of the young lads from the region who had escaped into the mountains to serve with the Maquis and of the pain some families suffered upon losing their sons, her focus was mostly on her daily routine, the food served, the food that was wanting, the annoyances brought on when electricity and telephone services were cut, and, as to be expected, the feelings of jubilation that followed "The Coming of the Americans" and the freeing of France. When Americans such as Eric Sevareid, the war correspondent whom Stein had met in Paris prior to the outbreak of hostilities, and Frank Gervasi of *Collier's*, discovered the whereabouts of this illustrious American, they were invited with pomp and circumstance to a "magnificent lunch." In his memoir, *Not So Wild a Dream*, Sevareid talks of Stein's nearly endless questions concerning the fate of so many of her friends both in Europe and in America. Still, he remarked, when it came to Pétain, he detected "a faint tone of sorrow" for the man. As for Hitler, she claimed he was "essentially a nineteenth century person" who succeeded in destroying the past. When Sevareid reminded her of the statement she had made to him prior to the war, that Hitler would present no threat since he was a German Romanticist who longed to experience the "illusion of power," but would certainly not resort to bloodshed to achieve his end, she did not answer. Rather, she resumed her chatter, thus avoiding the admission of so grave an error on her part. After accepting Sevareid's invitation to broadcast to America, she told her audiences—now that the war was over and fears past—what she knew *they wanted to hear.*

I can tell you that liberty is the most important thing in the world more important than food or clothes, more important than anything on this mortal earth, I who spent four years with the French under the German yoke tell you so. I am so happy to be talking to America today so happy.[88]

Upon her return to Paris, Stein breathed a sigh of relief when she found most all of her precious possessions intact. Picasso, who had been informed about some items that had been taken during the occupation—a footstool for which he had designed the cover, a pair of Louis XIV silver candlesticks, and other items— called Bernard Fay, who told him not to worry. He would see to the safety of Stein's things. Stein called it a "miracle" and Bernard Fay, the German collaborator, had been the miracle worker.

The days to follow were joyous for Stein. She saw old friends, including Hemingway, who was now a war correspondent. They had reconciled. Her home on rue Christine became the meeting ground for American soldiers stationed in Europe. Some were incipient writers who asked her to read and comment on their work, others just wanted to talk with her about the old days, and still others felt at home with this American in Paris. Stein by now had become a legendary figure.

In 1945 Stein and Toklas were flown to US Army bases in Germany, Salzburg, Frankfurt, and even Berchtesgarden. Stein described her impressions in an article for *Life* magazine, "Off We All Went to See Germany."[89] Upon her return to Paris, she began *Brewsie and Willie,* a shallow work about American soldiers in Europe, exploring the special language they used, their needs, joys, longings, and including as well her own views, meditations, and "prognostications" about the world to come.

Stein lectured to the American GIs stationed in Brussels, then traveled to Biarritz to oversee the production of her play, *Yes Is for a Very Young Man*. She also wrote a libretto to Thomson's music: *The Mother of Us All*. Its theme revolved around the suffragette, Susan B. Anthony.

Although she was still active, Stein's strength was ebbing. She no longer had the zest, the drive, or resiliency she once had. She tired quickly and easily became cranky. Repeated intestinal problems plagued her. She was advised to consult a specialist. She did not. Her fatigue increased. She lost weight for no apparent reason.

No longer interested in the presence of American soldiers in Paris, she at times uttered the most unfeeling and thoughtless statements. For example, she told the young American writer, James Lord, that it saddened her to think that once the soldiers would "go home and take off their army uniforms and be done with the war and the army, they would never again in their lives be so happy." Lord thought differently. To her statement that soldiers would look back on their wartime experiences "all their lives with pleasure and nostalgia because they had been carefree among other men and because men loved fighting," he countered no: the men "were sick of the war, sick of the army." Stein complained that he was unaware of the situation, whereupon he called her a "stupid old woman who didn't understand anything." When he repeated her remarks to Picasso that very same day, the painter called her "a real Fascist. She always had a weakness for Franco. Imagine! For Pétain, too. You know she wrote speeches for Pétain. Can you imagine it? An American. A Jewess, what's more."[90]

Mention must also be made of the many letters Stein wrote to the authorities on behalf of Bernard Fay, who had been imprisoned for collaboration. After escaping from prison, he went to Spain, then to Switzerland, and was pardoned in 1957. When Stein decided to go to rest away from Paris, it was Fay who offered her his home in Indre-et-Loire. Since it was too far from Paris, a friend drove her and Toklas to Azay-le-Rideau. It was there, at an inn, that Stein took ill. A doctor was called, examined her, and told her to consult a specialist. The train ride back to Paris was difficult. Stein paced up and down the car. The awaiting ambulance, ordered by her nephew, Allan Stein, took her directly to the American Hospital at Neuilly. Surgery was ordered. She made out her will: Picasso's painting of her would go to the Metropolitan Museum of Art in New York City; her manuscripts and papers to the Yale University library. The executors of her will would pay Carl Van Vechten the money needed for the publication of her unpublished manuscripts. The rest of her possessions and money would go to Toklas as long as she lived and, after her death, to her nephew, Allan Stein, and upon his demise to his children.

Although the surgeons wanted to wait for Stein to grow stronger before operating on her, her pain was so intense that they decided not to delay. Moments before being taken to the operating room and already under heavy sedation, she said to Toklas who was at her bedside, "What is the question?" Before a reply could be given, she continued, "If there is no question then there is no answer."[91] During the surgery, which took place on July 27, 1946, they discovered that the cancer had already metastasized. At 5:30 Stein was comatose. An hour later, she was dead.

Stein was buried on October 22, 1946. Despite the fact that she had been a nonpracticing Jew, Toklas took it upon herself to have "special ceremonies" held at the American Cathedral Church of the Holy Trinity in Paris, where Stein's body, to the shock and consternation of friends and relatives, remained for several months until space could be found in Père Lachaise Cemetery, the burying place of so many great French artists, writers, and composers.

Toklas lived on, alone, feeding on memories and writing *The Alice B. Toklas Cookbook* (1954) and her memoirs, *What Is Remembered* (1963). She converted to Catholicism in 1958. Thomson remarked that, in so doing, she was assured of an afterlife that she would spend with her beloved. As for Stein, who had never believed in a hereafter, he suggested that the entire incident must have made her chuckle from wherever she was, for it was she who had stated categorically, and repeatedly throughout her life, that *Dead is Dead*.[92]

Toklas died on March 7, 1967. She was buried in the same tomb as Stein. Leo died of cancer on July 27, 1947, at the age of seventy-four.

Part II

The Work

What is poetry and if you know what poetry is what is prose.

There is no use in telling more than you know, no not even if you do not know it.

But do you do you know what prose is and do you know what poetry is.

—Gertrude Stein, "Poetry and Grammar,"
Lectures in America

2

ᤒᤒᤒᤒᤒᤒᤒᤒᤒᤒᤒᤒᤒᤒᤒᤒᤒᤒᤒᤒᤒᤒᤒᤒᤒᤒᤒᤒᤒᤒᤒᤒᤒᤒ

The Matriarch and Her Lover

"Do you think that Alice and I are lesbians?" Stein asked an American friend a few years before the outbreak of World War II. "Do you care whether we are?"[1]

Never would Stein have spoken so openly about lesbianism at the turn of the century. Restrained about her sexual proclivities, she controlled any natural outpouring on this forbidden subject in the puritanical world that was the Radcliffe and the Johns Hopkins of her day. At least publicly, "restraint of course was part of the times then. But naturally I was ashamed of it."[2]

The island of Lesbos populated by Amazonian women in ancient times, was "a sacred colony dedicated to worship of the female principle, as later Christian monasteries were dedicated to worship of the male."[3] By the sixth century B.C., Lesbos was dominated by women serving such Great Mothers as Aphrodite and Artemis, through perfection of music, art, dancing, poetry, philosophy, and *Lesbian* love. When Judeo-Christian patriarchal or phallocentric societies banned lesbianism as a crime, its sinners went underground.

In her environment, when Stein understood her lesbian tendencies, she experienced feelings of extreme guilt. Such distress is clearly evident in her novella. "Q.E.D." (1903). Were friends or relatives to read this fictional, yet autobiographical work, they would be shocked, she felt, and she would be discredited in their eyes. At twenty-nine years of age, Stein did not feel strong enough to brave custom or tradition, so she slipped the manuscript into a drawer and promptly forgot about it. When, in 1931, she showed it to Louis Bromfield, who encouraged her to have it published despite the "great difficulties" such an admission might involve, she again decided against publication, fearing Toklas would be deeply hurt by its contents. (Toklas, as has been mentioned, had it published in 1950, only after Stein's death.)

Outside of her brother, her professors, and a few intellectual male friends, Stein did not have what is referred to as a boyfriend. Nor did she respond to men sexually. She enjoyed discussions with them, becoming highly argumentative and even aggressive when seeking to win a point. Nor did her girth, her slovenliness, her disinterestedness in clothes, her bellowing laughter, her strong and at times loud voice, endear her to the opposite sex. Stein seemed to be oblivious to these factors. Her *mind,* she knew from the start, was that single powerful weapon upon which she could count. It enabled her to do well in her courses when she chose to. All in her world seemed calculated and determined by conscious choice on her part.

Leo represented the only security she had. A father figure, she admired him for his knowledge on subjects about which she was not well informed: history, philosophy, art. He was her mentor, particularly after moving to Paris. She, his docile pupil. There was, however, that other side of her personality that longed for independence and resented her brother's dominance. It cried out to be on its own. Unconsciously, she projected feelings of hatred onto Leo, rejecting him for her own deficiencies. She recognized her inability to function as an individual, but then, how could she? Who was she? Questions of identity and of gender were always cropping up. What was she? Man? Woman? Where did she fit in? Or did she fit in at all?

When Leo was a student at Hopkins, brother and sister shared an apartment. Although each worked at his and her specialty, they lived a symbiotic relationship. Leo was the mentor who preached freedom from convention to Stein and her friends who visited: Emma Loots, Mabel Weeks, and others, all intent on liberating themselves from their Quaker traditions. After Leo's departure for Europe, Stein continued his work, more aggressively perhaps than had her soft-toned brother; and perhaps because of her naïveté and lack of experience, she was caught in her own trap.

Stein used to attend the teas of two highly sophisticated and well-to-do Bryn Mawr graduates, Mabel Haynes and Grace Lounsbury, who shared an apartment. Smith college graduates were also invited. But from the very start, Stein felt like an outsider—not intellectually, but experientially. What she took to be their

"Raw virginity!" was in fact her own.[4] She thought them naïve, when in reality they were highly sophisticated both sexually and emotionally. She misunderstood the kind of relationships these girls enjoyed among themselves. When Mabel Haynes, for example, grew tired of Miss Lounsbury, she turned her affections to May Bookstaver. Nor was Stein aware of the fact that economics played a role in their association. Not only did Mabel pay May's bills, but she took her on trips to Europe and Boston. Only when Stein herself fell in love with May did she realize that May, to all intents and purposes, was a kept woman.

The autobiographical nature of "Q.E.D." became evident when it was discovered that actual sentences from Stein's correspondence with May had been transcribed into the text of her novella. The shame she felt when realizing her "passion" for May had a sickening effect on her. A puritanical upbringing had not only repressed Stein's sexual needs, but had allowed her life to remain "unlived." Both fearful of and eager to learn about lesbian love, particularly since she had come to adore May, the text reads: "I could undertake to be an efficient pupil if it were possible to find an efficient teacher." Instead of taking her under her wing, May laughed at her. Understandably, Stein bled from such a hurt. Yet pain, when experienced and explored, may have a healing effect if it serves to expand knowledge.

Stein's passion for May encouraged her to explore the differences between them, assessing her beloved's approach to life as follows: "You are Anglo-Saxon, brave, passionate but not emotional, capable of great sacrifice but not tenderhearted." She, on the other hand, was introverted and unsure of herself, without the physical beauty, wealth and class of her friends, and, therefore could not hope to compete with them. It was crucial that she find her own way through mentation. The drive to *understand* people's needs—and by extension her own—encouraged her to dissect her feelings as she had the cadavers in medical school. "I am a hopeless coward, I hate to risk hurting myself or anybody else. All I want to do is to meditate endlessly and think and talk."[5] There were periods when the hurt so overwhelmed her that it aroused inordinate antagonism for her rival, Mabel, thereby preventing any integration of the polarities that were tearing her apart. Each time May fell under Mabel's spell, Stein felt herself exiled from her love, an outsider, *belonging* to no one, fragmented, and bewildered.

Stein's trips to Europe during the summers of 1901 and 1902 did not solve her problems. In fact, they exacerbated them. She was greeted by May upon her return with accusations of "brutality." Periods of depression ensued. Even after Stein surrendered to her instinct and sexual enjoyment was experienced, the love and security she sought from such a relationship were not forthcoming. May neither wanted nor needed these things. Their "rhythms" were at variance and "their pulses were differently timed." Did such a comment suggest frigidity on Stein's part? Stein withdrew from the relationship that was never really one, and perhaps for this reason even sought exile from America. To sever the umbilical cord might deliver her from the trauma she had just endured.

What Stein had learned only intellectually in courses on psychology, medicine, and research work had now been experienced in real life. Henceforth, she realized she would have to learn to cope with her idiosyncratic ways, her unchanneled feelings, even while attempting to carve out a future for herself. Understandably, her interests were directed to the study of human relationships, their meaning, and their consequences for her.

"Q.E.D." was perhaps a means of self-therapy under the guise of fiction, capable of exorcising the sense of utter rejection Stein experienced in the aftermath of her first real love affair. Her inquiry into her needs drew her to ponder the question as to whether May had ever *really* returned her love or whether it had merely been a passing escapade? Did she even know the meaning of the emotion of love?

As an inveterate reader of Henry James, George Eliot, Samuel Richardson, and Shakespeare, Stein was, understandably, influenced by some of their literary techniques. Her opening quotation, used to set the tone of her novella, came from *As You Like It.* Unlike James and Eliot, Stein does away with all description of landscape, environment, background material, depiction of fineries, in order better to concentrate on the psychological types she seeks to understand. Like James, however, Stein creates a central consciousness, always alert to the events and advents taking place, and when need be participates in their direction. Like the French naturalists, Stein is a determinist: the psychology of her characters not only makes their actions predictable, but serves to mechanize the orchestration of their sensations and feelings. Like Richardson and Joris-Karl Huysmans, particularly in *Against the Grain,* there is not a thought, discussion, or misunderstanding to which the reader is not made privy, perhaps accounting somewhat for the tedium and circularity of "Q.E.D." On the other hand, such an approach serves to distance Stein from her protagonists, while also inviting her to sound out their hermetic inner worlds. Is it any wonder that "Q.E.D." concludes as follows: "I am afraid it comes very near being a dead-lock."

That Stein uses the geometrical figure of a triangle as a paradigm of her protagonists' vagaries indicates the need to dissect the emotional world via the safety and relative predictability of a mathematical/scientific point of view. Only by objectifying and categorizing could she, seemingly, begin to understand and then cope with the turbulent inner emotional sea that must be confronted during the life experience. Yet, in conflict with Stein's willfully programmed static figure of the triangle is the Pythagorean's understanding of this same mathematical image: as fire and heart. The inclusion of both outlooks—the triangle, representing the static nature of Stein's genetically programmed character types, and its Pythagorean opposite, the fire/heart aspect of the human personality engendered by the play of emotions—makes for a broad-based analysis.

The triangular motif is also clearly embedded in the very structure of "Q.E.D." It is made up of three sections each named after three distinct personality types: Adele (Stein: articulate, meditative, and sensual), Mabel Neathe (Mabel Haynes: puritanical, unfeeling, and materialistic), and Helen Thomas (May Bookstaver: emotional and weakly structured), the love object of the other two; three ocean voyages; three years of action time; and the completion of the work in 1903.

"Q.E.D." begins with Adele, the narrator, and her two traveling companions, Helen and Mabel, aboard a steamer en route to Europe. The locus of the action is not only autobiographical but is psychologically illuminating as well. Water, the very source of life and regeneration, also symbolizes the unconscious: those unformed emotions and feelings that activate humans, thus paving the way for certain relationships to form, blossom, and disintegrate. As the germ for all development and possibilities, the insights into personality offered the reader during the course of the voyage and throughout the novella are multiple: Helen, "the American version of the english handsome girl," was a "woman of passions but not of emotions, capable of long sustained action,

incapable of regrets." Mabel revealed an "attitude of awkward
discomfort and the tension of her long angular body sufficiently
betrayed her New England origin." As for Adele, she "had
thrown herself prone on the deck with the freedom of movement
and the simple instinct for comfort that suggested a land of lazi-
ness and sunshine."

Sensual, certainly, Adele is first and foremost a woman of
ideas. Discussions that she develops, cast in her role as supreme
consciousness, revolve around concepts of truth and virtue and
class consciousness: "You don't realise the important fact that
virtue and vice have it in common that they are vulgar when not
passionately given"—an idea Stein would maintain for years to
come.

Adele conveyed the changes she observed in her relationship
with Helen in the following way:

In the chilly evenings as Adele lay at her side on the deck, Helen would
protect her from the wind and would allow her hand to rest gently on
her face and her fingers to flutter vaguely near her lips. At such times
Adele would have dimly a sense of inward resistance, a feeling that if she
were not so sluggish she would try to decide whether she should yield or
resist but she felt too tired to think, to yield or to resist and so she lay
there quite quiet, quite dulled.

The next evening, however, as she lay on her berth,

she suddenly awakened out of her long emotional apathy. For the first
time she recognised the existence of Helen's consciousness and realised
how completely ignorant she was both as to its extent and its meaning.
She meditated a long time.

Helen is an enigma for Adele. Does she really care for her?
Helen's remark—"I am afraid that after all you haven't a nature
much above passionettes" and suggests she is fearful of losing her
"moral sense"—sets her thinking. When Helen begins pressing
her hand "gently over her [Adele] eyes," Adele longs for the security of commitment, which is not forthcoming: "Care for you my
dear, more than you know and less than you think." Looking at
the stars one evening, Adele "felt herself intensely kissed on the
eyes and on the lips." Her inhibitions lead her to mask her intense
joy, by calling upon her intellect: "I was just thinking." Helen

now focuses on the very core of Adele's problem: "Haven't you ever stopped thinking long enough to feel?"

The second and third parts of "Q.E.D." take place in the United States. Mabel, domineering and aggressive, seeks, but fails "to take effective hold on the objects of her desire." Adele's growing resentment of Mabel's "ownership" of Helen and her growing adoration of her love-object add tension to the novella. Only at the conclusion does she realize that she must adjust, changing her standards and values in the process.

Although Stein identifies with Adele, she also possesses, in a still-dormant state, characteristics linking her to both Helen and Mabel. The complexity of her personality is brought out with insight by Helen, who despite what she felt to be Adele's "inveterate egotism" was the only person with whom she could "ever come into close contact" and continue to respect.

I realise always one whole you consisting of a laugh so hard that it rattles, a voice that suggests a certain brutal coarseness and a point of view that is aggressively unsympathetic, and all that is one whole you and it alternates with another you that possesses a purity and intensity of feeling that leaves me quite awestruck and a gentleness of voice and manner and an infinitely tender patience that entirely overmasters me. Now the question is which is really you because these two don't seem to have any connections.

Receiving Helen's assurance, "Oh you stupid child, don't you realise that you are the only thing in the world that makes anything seem real or worthwhile to me," Adele glimpses a momentary flickering. In one of their confessional interludes, when Helen's kiss "seemed to scale the very walls of chastity," she battles with feelings of revulsion. Greatly embarrassed, she tells her she never realized that she was still "such a virgin soul" and begs her forgiveness, explaining that her puritan instincts make her feel degraded under such circumstances. She also becomes aware of the fact that she cannot respond to Helen's lovemaking as rapidly as her lover wants her to, the implication being that her orgasms are slow in coming. "Their pulses were differently timed. She could not go so fast and Helen's exhausted nerves could no longer wait." Adele, evidently, had to learn to transcend the "Calvinistic influence that dominates American training," and that blocks her natural temperament. After some misunderstandings

and reconciliations, Adele withdraws from the triangle, aware of
Helen's inability to give her the security and solace she so desperately needs.

Although Stein emerged scarred from her unhappy love experience she, like Adele, understood that she would have to learn to
cope with her idiosyncrasies: her inhibitions, her possessiveness,
and her need for continuous assurances of love, even while attempting to carve out a future for herself. A composite of the
three protagonists, she was, like Adele, timid, puritanical, and interested in things of the mind; like Mabel, she was domineering
and seeking to be the center of attention; like Helen, she feared
alienating people because she was in such desperate need of them.

Stein's striking and bold intuitions in her character depictions
were commented upon by Edmund Wilson, who pointed out her
"astonishing lack of self-consciousness" and her profound understanding of the human personality.[6]

So depressed did Stein feel while composing "Q.E.D." that she
began keeping notebooks, setting down her feelings, thoughts, reactions, and a multitude of quotations gleaned from her many
readings covering English narrative from the fifteenth to the nineteenth centuries. According to Leon Katz, her despair over her
abortive love affair with May was so great that during her first
four years in Paris, "[S]he became passive, cynical; she was
moved to do nothing." Her notebooks and letters do not paint the
picture of an excited and passionate devotee of the arts that is
depicted in her *Autobiography of Alice B. Toklas*. On the contrary, she was "sorrowful and debilitated. . . . The joyous, over-
whelmingly confident Stein of Hopkins days had altogether
disappeared."[7]

Although distressing, the writing of "Q.E.D." was catalytic for
Stein. The emotional detritus that lay fallow within her had been
partially expelled. It took another fictional work, the novella
"Fernhurst," also based on a triangular love relationship, to rid
her even more profoundly of her sense of guilt and worthlessness.
("Fernhurst" was later revised and included in *The Making of
Americans*.)

The novella is based on the scandalous affair that took place at
Bryn Mawr in 1898 between Helen Carey Thomas (Miss Thorn-
ton), the authoritarian, pitiless, and possessive dean of Bryn
Mawr; Mary Gwinn (Janet Bruce), the object of her love—

charming, easily dominated, and highly prized lecturer who had "set the tone of Bryn Mawr's intellectual life"; Alfred Hodder (Redfern), the brilliant and romantic Harvard-educated philosophy professor; and his wife (Nancy), naive, unable to understand her husband's complex personality. Hoddard finally asked his wife for a divorce and married Miss Gwinn. Both left Bryn Mawr in 1904 and went to Paris, where they visited the Steins whom they had known since their Harvard days.[8] It was Bertrand Russell who informed the anxious gossip mongers that Hodder died not too long after his marriage, exhausted from his intemperate ways.

In Stein's "Fernhurst," the triangle was transformed into a square, suggesting a concomitant psychological change occurring in herself. A geometric symbol, the square represents the conflation of earth and matter and stability and balance within the personality. One has the distinct feeling, in reading "Fernhurst," that although Stein still grieves for her lost love, writing has become her salvation. The creative principle, an active and positive factor in her life, has become the weapon enabling her to *struggle* through despondency and depression.

Seemingly, Stein identified with Nancy Redfern, the naive, confused, well wisher married to a womanizer. Unable to assess her husband's passion for Miss Gwinn when it was still a rumor, and utterly defenseless once it had become fact, so Stein was blinded when discovering her lover's materialism. That Nancy returned to her father, as Stein had to her brother, seeking comfort in him who had been her mentor, indicated regression on her part, but also a desire to seek healing. In "Fernhurst," Redfern does not marry Miss Bruce, because she was unable to break with Miss Thornton, so dependent upon her had she become. "Patiently and quietly the dean worked it out and before many years she had regained all property rights in this shy learned creature." As for Redfern, he was forced to resign from the college. While "Q.E.D." concluded in a "dead-lock," "Fernhurst" alludes to Redfern's last hour on earth—psychologically, the death of that weakly structured element within his psyche. Rather than withdraw from the struggle, which is what Stein had done when leaving for Europe, she now intentionally kills that continuously unproductive aspect that lives within her via projection. By doing away with Redfern, we are given a premonitory image of Stein's growing emotional strength: her ability—though it would still take months and even years to develop—to destroy the last vestiges of May's stranglehold over her.

What makes "Fernhurst" relevant for today's reader are the problems that confront college girls, particularly those studying at private institutions. Intellect, athletics, and accomplishments have been stressed during their four years at college. But then, as Stein remarks: "Much the same as a man's work if you like before he becomes a man but how much different from a man's work when manhood has once been attained." Upon graduation, the young lady finds herself at a crossroad: she faces a gender problem (she must "relearn the fundamental facts of sex") and an identity crisis. Where does she go from here? To a career? To the home? How can she combine both satisfactorily and still be a good mother—that is, if she chooses to have children at all?

Stein's next work, written in a relatively conventional style, yet concretizing certain character traits, *Three Lives* marks Stein's stylistic breakthrough into what would eventually become her own innovative literary course. Of the three short stories included in the volume, the second, "Melanctha," is the most revolutionary. She rids her prose of continuous and logically sequenced action; indulges in consistent and mannered repetitions, thus not only pointing up the fluidity of human relationships and emotions, but also setting up intricate rhythmic effects that serve to haunt and mesmerize the reader. The other two tales, "The Good Anna" and "The Gentle Lena" are more traditional in nature.

Although Stein pointed to Gustave Flaubert's influence when composing *Three Lives*, there is little evidence of his artistry or technique in any of these tales. The author of *Madame Bovary*, who spent years researching every possible document that might yield information about his protagonists; who agonized over every word until he struck the *one* that would exactly convey his intent, was a writer of different ilk. In Stein's stories, no detailed picture of the milieu was offered; nor was she obsessed with the notion of exactitude. Although both were interested in style, Flaubert opted for concision, plot, suspense, and analogical devices linking the disparate to the whole; Stein focused on incision and stylized repetition, multiple personifications—a technique designed to impress and arouse the reader's sensate world. Thus, in her case, words, recurring phrases, and clauses take on a hypnotic, even a ritualistic effect. That Stein's protagonists in all three stories were maids does make them analogous to the character in Flaubert's "A Simple Heart." The maids portrayed in Stein's stories were inspired by those who had worked for her and her brother when they were at Johns Hopkins; from Flaubert, she may have learned to define character types more succinctly in a phrase ("The good Anna was a small, spare, german woman"), or in a sentence ("Lena was patient, gentle, sweet and german").

Cézanne's influence, Stein had said, was also implicit in her new writing style. In fact, when composing *Three Lives*, she sat beneath the *Portrait of Madame Cézanne*. Her use of the triangle and the square in "Q.E.D." and in "Fernhurst" became accentuated in *Three Lives*. Her intent (and Cézanne's) was to "recreate" nature by simplifying forms right down to their basic geometric equivalents. In so doing, Stein developed new narrative spatial patterns within which her characters circumambulated, stopped to rest, talk, sorrow, struggle, love, inviting readers to observe them from continuously shifting vantage points. While Stein's repeated use of words, designed to accent altering insights, distort tone and tempi, they also convey moods and penetrate the very essence of character. Also like Cézanne, she took to painting verbal portraits of her characters, varying the sequence and placement of recurring words and phrases ever so slightly, while concomitantly altering the tonalities and rhythms of the figures involved, thus enabling her to convey the emotions and sensations of the *moment*. Although only implicit in "The Good Anna" and "The Gentle Lena," such a technique is explicit in "Melanctha," in which vibrating interrelationships continuously act on her characters' inner and outer worlds, or planes, to use Cézanne's words. Stein, like the painter, also attempts to bring order to her portrayals and not approach them randomly. She courageously carries Cézanne's dictum—"that in composition one thing was as important as another thing"—into the literary field, ridding her tales as much as possible of plot and a focal point around which suspense or the entire composition revolved.[9]

The reader, viewing the routine comings and goings in the home as "The Good Anna," a zealous housekeeper who forces those under her aegis to work hard, listens to multiple voices and accents of the foreigners who congregate in the home. Class distinctions are also implied—those existing between the leisured and the hardworking groups. Banalities are uttered by the personages lending an authentic ring to their character. The awkwardness in some of Stein's phrases and sentences is an example of the frequent infelicities as she sets her new compositional technique into motion. When Lena finally dies from a "hard" operation, her exhausted body unable to fight for life, the sociorealistic element in the short story comes forward, a vestige of nineteenth- rather than twentieth-century literary practice.

A gem of its kind, "The Gentle Lena" is comparable in its sensitivity and terse dialogue to the works of Stephen Crane and George Eliot. Lena, who seeks kindness throughout life, finds herself the victim of a domineering aunt who, against her wishes, marries her off to the equally recalcitrant Herman. In time, they both adjust to their situation and lead a relatively harmonious life until Lena dies after having given birth to her fourth child.

Although there is more plot in "The Gentle Lena" than in "The Good Anna," there are greater stylistic innovations in the former: interior indirect discourse and monologue, and examples of what Stein will call a "prolonged present." Defined as discourse that, by dint of repetition, expands and elongates time, while revolving around itself in slow, circular, and extended passages, the concept of "continuous present" invites the reader and protagonist to journey in time from the past forward. In the following passage, a paradigm of Stein's *continuous present*, Herman's father prevails upon him to marry Lena:

You like all young people Herman, you think only about yourself, and what you are just wanting, and your mama she is thinking only what is good for you to have, for you in the future. Do you think your mama wants to have a girl around to be a bother, for herself, Herman. It's just for you herman she is always thinking, and she talks always about how happy she will be, when she sees her Herman married to a nice girl, and then when she fixed it all up so good for you, so it never would be any bother to you, just the right way she wanted you should like it, and you say yes all right, I do it, and then you go away like this and act stubborn, and make all this trouble everybody to take for you, and we spend money, and I got to travel all around to find you.

"Melanctha" marks Stein's stylistic breakthrough and is regarded as one of the first naturalistic treatments of blacks by a white person. The syntactical devices Stein uses to probe the psyches of her characters, recorded in black English, are authentic. By expunging her story as much as possible of personal references—unsatisfactory relationships that mirror her own—by fragmenting her sequences and characterizations, Stein eliminates narrative linearity, and in so doing, lends her tale a universal flavor. Stein's *continuous present*, though used at times in "The Gentle Lena," is implicit in "Melanctha's" very structure. The present, she believes, is the only valid time; the past is significant only in terms of how it relates to present moods, feelings, and events.

One can delve more deeply into a human being's psyche, Stein noted, through the repetition of words, actions, thoughts, and behavioral patterns in a *present* setting. The use of a *continuous present*, therefore, allows readers to view fragments of a life, drawn from past, present, and future time frames, thus yielding greater insights into the character. The character may be considered a unified entity in that he or she contains *all* the moments made manifest verbally in the work. Stein's use of the present participle rather than the perfect, which indicates a completed action in the past, serves also to accentuate her trust in the powers of the continuous present.

Melanctha Herbert, the protagonist, a sexually active servant girl, falls in love with a black doctor, Jefferson Campbell. The analysis of their developing and declining love and the emotions involved fascinates Stein, interested as she was in psychological types. After Campbell and Melanctha leave each other, she begins a liaison with the irresponsible Jem Richards, which also terminates unhappily. In time and after much turmoil, and perhaps even incurring Stein's boredom with it all now that she has probed the multiple layers of human feeling, Melanctha dies of consumption.

Stein's expert use of the continuous present succeeds in fleshing out the inner workings of her personalities through repetitions, to be sure, but also by making good use of assonances and inner rhymes that serve to accentuate the series of cumulative movements and emotions these arouse. The reader can *feel* Jeff's tension as he ruminates in a confrontational pattern between past and present:

These months had been an uncertain time for Jeff Campbell. He never knew how much he really knew about Melanctha. He saw her now for long times and very often. He was beginning always more and more to like her. But he did not seem to himself to know very much about her.

He was beginning to feel he could almost trust the goodness in her. But then, always, really, he was not very sure about her. Melanctha always had ways that made him feel uncertain, and yet, he was so near, in his feeling for her. He now never thought about all this in real words any more. He was always letting it fight itself out in him. He was now never taking any part in the fighting that was always going on inside him.

Repetition and the use of the continuous present becomes a stylistic device to depict Melanctha's sexual activity, with men or women, which always ends unhappily or, at best, in a stalemate.

Jane grew always fonder of Melanctha. Soon they began to wander, more to be together than to see men and learn their various ways of working. Then they began not to wonder, and Melanctha would spend long hours with Jane in her room, sitting at her feet and listening to her stories, and feeling her strength and the power of her affection, and slowly she began to see clear before her one certain way that would be sure to lead to wisdom.

What is of import in "Melanctha" is not the event, which is minimal, but the cumulative movements experienced by the protagonists when passionately involved with either a man or a woman. Instead of the obvious and relatively superficial manner in which love and jealousy motifs were intellectualized in "Q.E.D." and "Fernhurst," in "Melanctha" they are depicted in great complexes of continuously shifting verbal planes. Nor are the protagonists delineated once and for all in virtually static configurations, but rather as kinetic forms, mobile tones, fragmented bits and pieces, living in a present time and voicing their pleasures and displeasures in sequences of detached conversations. Thus did Stein take to heart in "Melanctha," Cézanne's suggestion to a student to present nature in its simplest and broadest dimensions.

Repetition, Stein remarked, also implies memory—the recalling of past events and feelings. When *what was* is reintegrated into *what is,* however, lapses and errors are also pointed up, thereby adding both tension and confusion to the scene. Melanctha, for example, a spontaneous and emotional individual, would like Jeff to "remember right," whereas he, introspective, ruminates about what he believes to have been said in the past. "Remember right just when it happens to you, so you have a right kind of feeling ... real feeling every moment when it's needed," Melanctha says to Jeff, urging him to experience the emotion immediately. She accuses her lover of being overly meditative and reflective, of systematizing and thinking too much about the past, thereby crippling his ability to act in the present. "When you ain't just that moment quick with feeling, then you certainly ain't ever got anything more there to keep you." Pursuing her argument, she affirms: "You don't remember nothing till you get home with your thinking everything all over." Indeed, because they function on different wavelengths, they each believe the other is not only incapable of recalling something correctly, but also of unconsciously distorting fact. The difference between reality and fiction, then, serves to increase an already complex and ambiguous set of feelings and sensations.

Although family backgrounds are clearly delineated, particularly Melanctha's and Jeff's, descriptive sequences are absent. Ambiguity still lies at the root of the protagonists' psychological makeup. Nothing is fixed. Nor are the beings incarnated. Voices emerge in a variety of rhythmic interludes and modulated clauses, devoid of physical accoutrements. Various consciousnesses converse in a medley of interacting abstractions, comparable in many respects to the disembodied creatures populating the works of Nathalie Sarraute and Samuel Beckett.

Although some reviewers found "Melanctha" condescending toward the black, Richard Wright, the author of *Black Boy,* came to Stein's defense, calling it "the first long serious literary treatment of Negro life in the United States." Moreover, he said that when he read it, "my ears were opened for the first time to the magic of the spoken word. I began to hear the speech of my grandmother, who spoke a deep, pure Negro dialect and with whom I had lived for many years."[10] When a left-wing literary critic wrote derogatorily about Stein's novella, implying she knew nothing about blacks since "she spent her days reclining upon a silken couch in Paris smoking hashish," Wright resorted to direct action: "I gathered a group of semi-literate Negro stockyard workers . . . into a Black Belt basement and read MELANCTHA aloud to them. They understood every word. Enthralled, they slapped their thighs, howled, laughed, stomped, and interrupted me constantly to comment upon the characters."[11]

By disguising her characters in codes and symbols used to define them, Stein still succeeded in hiding her lesbianism. In *Two: Ger-*

trude Stein and Her Brother (1908–12), she not only depicted sequences of homosexual couples visiting 27, rue de Fleurus—and
perhaps of herself and her apparently bisexual brother—but also
the transferences that had occurred after Toklas had entered their
household.

Two is a stylistic feat. Stein uses words connoting *sound* (repeated in every paragraph throughout nearly half of the book) to
emphasize hearing/listening, and communication, once so acute a
part of her relationship with her brother, and subsequently turned
sour. Sound, however, is not merely a literary device: it is also
grounded in reality, since Leo was actually growing increasingly
deaf. Repetitions are also cleverly used. Their interlocking variations and displacements in the text succeed in pointing up complex rhythmic effects designed to underscore the minute changes
in relationships and the concomitant tensions to which they give
rise. Such verbal, tonal, and metered patternings also serve as an
analytical device enabling Stein to highlight the "bottom nature"
of her characters—their essence. As she pursues her probings, the
beat of the continuously recurring regular and irregular placement of words bores ever more deeply into the personalities under
scrutiny. A slow erosion of their customary defenses begins—the
social masks people don to prevent the outside world from looking into their very secret realm. Stein, the psychologist, the scientist is in full control.[12]

Two, although considered dull and repetitious by some readers,
should nevertheless be studied as a verbal exercise, allowing readers to gain insight into the riches Stein brought to writing, which
Sarraute, Michel Butor, Robbe-Grillet, would later fashion in
other ways. *Two* is an important step that Stein took to assure her
own development as a writer.

Stein's "Ada," a verbal portrait of Toklas (1908) discloses in hermetic terms Stein's involvement with her lover. By changing the
name from Alice to "Ada," Stein succeeds in depersonalizing her
subject while also retaining certain factual information. Although
seemingly impersonal, "Ada" is highly subjective as it decodes the
extraordinary happiness and contentment Stein enjoys with Toklas. Moved by her lover's extreme consideration and devotion to
her, in sharp contrast to the pain she suffered at the hands of
May, feelings are conveyed, as they were in *Two*, by means of
interlocking repetition, alliteration, assonance, and metered pat-

ternings. "Trembling was all living, living was all loving, some one was then the other one. Certainly this one was loving this Ada then. And certainly Ada all her living then was happier in living than any one else who ever could, who was, who is, who ever will be living."[13]

Stein could not help but react in the most positive manner to Toklas's devotion. That she typed her virtually illegible manuscripts; listened patiently as she read her writings to her; and called her a "genius," a term she had always applied to herself, were impressed in her word portrait of her lover.

That one who was loving was almost always listening. That one who was loving was telling about being one then listening. That one being loving was then telling stories having a beginning and a middle and an ending.

After Leo's departure from 27, rue de Fleurus, Stein was free to be herself, to establish a matriarchate and become its ruling feminine power. As her friendship and love for Toklas deepened, profounder layers of her psyche became involved, opening her up to an all-embracing emotional experience. Certainly, at the outset of their relationship, Stein alluded to what could be interpreted as Toklas's sexual reticence or frigidity toward her. In time, however, her repressed sexuality was finally constellated along with the recognition and acceptance of her lesbianism. By working out their differences together and in all honesty, they seemingly had strengthened their love and mutual confidence in each other.

"Lifting Belly" (1915), a fifty-page poem, was written during World War I, when Stein and Toklas spent long months in Majorca. In what has come to be known as *Steinese,* its style involves elliptically and cryptically phrased love sequences, patterned repetitions, even and uneven beats, vocal harmonies and cacophonies, depending upon the momentary temper of the protagonists. Interwoven into the text are seemingly homey comments concerning the combing of hair, the cooking of food, the nature of animals and plants, bouts of possessiveness, rapture, and anger. Within the outwardly daily trivia reported in the lines of this intentionally disparate and fragmented work, are intimations, illusions, and outright references to the sexual pleasures Stein experiences and to the expertise she uses in delighting her partner. Be it with reference to the cooking of food, the picking of a flower, or the image of "lifting belly," the viscerality and rythmicality of the overt act is analogized to an orgasmic experience.[14]

> Lifting belly is so adaptable.
> That will amuse my baby.
> Lifting belly is so strong. I love cherish idolise adore and
> worship you. You are so sweet so tender and so perfect.
> Kiss my lips. She did
> Kiss my lips again she did.
> Kiss my lips over and over and over again she did.
>
> Lifting belly all around.
> Eat the little girl I say.
> Listen to me. Did you expect it to go back. Why do you do to stop.

The repetitions and rhythmic techniques in "Lifting Belly" are cumulative and analogical—designed to swell until a climax is reached, then subside, their intensity diminishing as contentment sets in.

Stein's continuous identification with foods, flowers, trees, animals, moisture of all types, adds a universal flavor to her sexual experience. It is in what has been termed a love idyll that Stein's famous line—to be interpreted metaphorically—appears: "Rose is a rose is a rose is a rose."

Although "Bee Time Vine and Other Pieces" is considered hermetic because it seeks "to describe a thing without mentioning it," its erotic inferences are at times quite obvious.

Such is sucking when there is a pack of sound which is goats which is lamb last lambling. Loaf. A hole is in seen and likely is to pudding when color is to buds. Buds when in seen solid, no coats, no black necessaries. A real kind is dew real cue act one.

In "A Sonatina Followed by Another," the sexuality of their relationship is even more explicit.[15]

The song of Alice B.
Little Alice B. is the wife for me. Little Alice B so tenderly is born so long so she can be born along by a husband strong who has not his hair shorn. And what size is wise. The right size is nice. How can you credit me with wishes. I wish you a very happy birthday.

How prettily we swim. Not in water. Not on land. But in love.

"As a Wife Has a Cow" is a love story for which Juan Gris created the lithographs (1926).[16] The image of the cow, used frequently by Stein, conveys her love and passion for Toklas, who, like the cow, the giver of milk, is a bountiful force in the life-giving and life-sustaining role she plays out in the poet's life.

Nearly all of it to be as a wife has a cow, a love story. All of it to be as a wife has a cow, all of it to be as a wife has a cow, a love story.

Stein's clever portrait, "Miss Furr and Miss Skeene," was modeled after Miss Mars and Miss Squire, relatively cultured Midwestern women who came to Paris at the turn of the century and whom Stein knew from their visits to her salon.[17] Although puritanical upon their arrival, after just one year in the liberating environment of the city of lights, the change in both of them was clearly discernible: they now sported brilliantly orange hair and heavy makeup, which looked more like a mask than a face. Miss Furr, who had left her husband because she was bored living in the same place, "was quite a pleasant woman." Their voices, which they cultivated, enhanced their popularity, as habitués of Parisian cafés. Although they sat with "some dark and heavy men," it is inferred that their pleasures were enjoyed with each other not with the opposite sex.

Helen Furr and Georgine Skeene were regularly living where very many were living and cultivating in themselves something. Helen Furr and Georgine Skeene were living very regularly then, being very regular then in being gay then, they did then learn many ways to be gay and they were then being gay being quite regular in being gay, being gay and they were learning little things, little things in ways of being gay, they were very regular then.

Although never explicitly stated, with the passing of years, their relationship floundered and then disintegrated. Each went her own way, each learning the art of love from others.

She came to using many ways in being gay, she came to use every way in being gay. She went on living where many were cultivating something and she was gay, she had used every way to be gay.

Sadness permeates the final sequence as both Miss Furr and Miss Skeene, old now, wander about like two shadows, two grotesque forms fading into oblivion.

The names Stein chose for her ladies, Furr and Skeene, may be viewed symbolically. The former, signifying an animal's pelt used as a coat or to line wearing apparel, may be thick, soft, and pleasant to rub. Like a fetish, it has sexual ramifications. Skeene, which brings to mind a skein, indicates a loosely coiled length of yarn or thread wound on a reel. It suggests the binding of a relationship, but also one filled with twists and contortions, tangles and knots. When unraveled, it leaves disarray in its wake.

Stein's repeated use of the motif "being gay" in "Miss Furr and Miss Skeene" and in other works, implies lesbianism, but also happiness and release—emotions neither woman had known when living in the Midwest. Stein's wordplay and fascination with the present participle, imparts the sensation of continuous action ("regular in being gay"), while ("being gay") casts a more limited spatiotemporal mood on the situation, as attested to in the analogy of interweaving yarn or interlocking relationships.

The typically Steinian internal rhyme schemes, which run through "Miss Furr and Miss Skeene" like a leitmotif adhering to ever-expanding associations of tones and metered devices, also serve to underscore the sexual activity implied by the *fur* and *skeene,* the ending of such bodily satisfaction, and the approach of tarnishing old age, which casts itself onto the two maiden ladies.[18]

3

xxxxxxxxxxxxxxxxxxxxxxxxxxxxxxxxxxxxxxxxxxxxxxxxxxxxxxxxxxxxxx

Verbal Portraits: Crosswords, CrossSections, Cross-purposes— Puzzling Logogriphs

Stein's writing not only explored psychological problems, but blended the pictorial as well as the verbal arts. Even while writing her novellas and her poems, she had also taken a fancy to creating verbal portraits:

And so I am trying to tell you what doing portraits meant to me, I had to find out what it was inside any one, and by any one I mean every one I had to find out inside every one what was in them that was intrinsically exciting and I had to find out not by what they said not by what they did not by how much or how little they resembled any other one but I had to find out by the intensity of movement that there was inside in any one of them.[1]

Verbal portraiture had a long tradition dating back to such ancients as Theophrastus and Aristotle, continuing through the Renaissance and reaching a high point in seventeenth-century France with La Bruyere and the language-oriented group known as *les précieuses:* Marquise de Rambouillet, Mlle. de Scudéry, and Mlle. de Montpensier. These and other noble ladies used to invite rhymemakers and clever prose writers to their salons to create literary portraits. Guests identifying the person depicted in the portrait would come away enthralled from this fashionable parlor game. Not so Molière, who, with pith and point, in his plays mocked the *précieuses'* pretentious literary genre.

Stein's claim to have been the inventor of the literary portrait is, despite the works of her predecessors, to a certain degree true.

She was the first to attempt the impossible: the fusion of pictorial and linguistic mediums.[2] Her goal was twofold: to express verbally and iconically the immediacy of a person's or an object's presence while also attempting to make manifest the direct sensations these triggered in her. Unlike those of many of her predecessors, Stein's literary portraits conveyed no moral or ideational values, no verbal concision or grammatically correct mannered images. Anti-mimetic in the traditional sense, but programmatic and structured—characteristics evident in *Two* and in "Melanctha"—the rhythms articulated were designed to suit the temperament of the characters portrayed. As in the above-mentioned works, Stein uses repetition and illogically sequenced clauses as a psychological device to point up the "bottom nature" of her human subject or nonhuman object.

The fusion of visual and literary spheres in Stein's verbal portraits led her to break new ground in this genre by doing away with nouns, whenever possible, and their referents involving memory, thus endowing the portrait, she claimed, with a static quality. Other parts of speech were used differently: as a means of obliterating any and all of language's sign-functions, thus making the reading and understanding of them quite difficult. In her lectures, "How to Write," "Poetry and Grammar," "Portraits and Repetition," Stein suggests relying on associational connections and internal and interlocking relationships as a sign of the person's or the object's immanence, rather than on traditional grammatical and syntactical order. Her goal of breaking up the usual syllogistic connections encouraged her to indulge in all sorts of puzzling logogriphs, wordplays, puns, non sequiturs, and convoluted rhythmic and tonal techniques. She hoped that her paradoxical verbal portraits would both create and release tension, heighten and slacken movement, arouse and mute sensation, even while assuring the immediacy of the experiencing in the ever-acting or ever-changing person or object depicted.

Time schemes are equally important and complex in Stein's literary portraits. The *continuous present,* defined in the preceding chapter, focuses on the *now* and the perception and "insistence" of sequenced and repetitive, but never identical, *nows.* Such a scheme again is paradoxical; it is also confusing, since to exist in the *now* implies dependency upon a past. Stein solves her dilemma by considering the metaphor of successive movie frames as a perpetual procession of *nows.*

By a continuously moving picture of any one there is no memory of any other thing and there is that thing existing it is in a way if you like one portrait of anything not a number of them.[3]

Just as no two pictures are ever alike in film, so they vary in Stein's verbal repetitions. By merely changing the place of a word in a clause, sentence, or paragraph, one alters its meaning, emphasis, and emotional impact.

By naming some of her portraits "Matisse," "Picasso," "Cézanne," Stein not only attracts attention to the individual, but also imbeds her subject's qualities and her reactions to them in her verbal referent. Some of her portraits are given fictitious names ("Ada") or, better still, names of streets ("Rue de Rennes") or department stores ("Galeries Lafayette"), or no names at all ("Fourteen Anonymous Portraits"). Strangely enough, no reference is made to the work of some of the people depicted. From her portrait of "Picasso," one might never guess that he was a painter. This is as it should be for Stein who, rather than evaluate her object cerebrally, logically, or mimetically, seeks to make the reader *aware* of the human presence via interrelationships on a variety of differing planes and through multiple referents. Drawing on her own vast lexicon and grammatical devices, she frequently endows her portraits with qualitative factors, thus paradoxically individualizing them through collective means.[4]

In Stein's verbal portrait "Matisse" (1908), she relates her version of his evolution and devolution as an artist. First, she seeks to convey the feelings of uncertainty, anxiety, and even terror accompanying the creative spirit in general setting out on an unknown quest. In so doing, she has recourse to what has become her trademark: untraditional syntax and indirect discourse. Via her continuous questioning technique and the repetition of the adjective *certain,* she triggers feelings of insecurity, tension, and irony, those very moods the artist must have experienced at the outset of his career.

One was quite certain that for a long part of his being one being-living he had been trying to be certain that he was wrong in doing what he was doing and then when he could not come to be certain that he had been wrong in doing what he had been doing, when he had completely convinced himself that he would not come to be certain that he had been wrong in doing what he had been doing he was really certain then that he was a great one and he certainly was a great one. Certainly every one could be certain of this thing that this one is a great one.

Word frequencies revolving around such clauses as, "one was quite certain," "he had been trying to be certain," "he could not come to be certain," create the wanted climate of malaise and of chaotic emotionality the painter feels during periods of crises.

Matisse is described as a "practical realist" in Stein's note-books—a man who paints "not from [Cézanne's and Picasso's] immediate contact with the object but from a passionate emotion about the object." Mention is made of Matisse's need for clarity and of "cleanness as an intellectual pictorial quality" as in Cézanne's canvases, which were for him paradigms of order and clarity. Indeed, as Matisse wrote: "For me all is in the concep-tion—I must have clear vision of the whole composition from the very beginning."[5]

The word *struggling,* which Stein uses throughout her portrait is the key to a deeper understanding of the man and his art. "Some said of him that he was greatly expressing something struggling. Some said of him that he was not greatly expressing something struggling." Since the concept of *struggling* is the sine qua non of every great artist, Matisse was compelled to grapple even more acutely to achieve clarity and order. "Some who came to know that of him, that he was a great one, that he was clearly expressing something, came then to be certain that he was not greatly expressing something being struggling." The very act of creation, which invites the rejection of the old and the imposition of the new, necessitates destruction of *what was* and thus fosters turmoil and confusion in its wake—the very elements Matisse was trying to transcend or at least integrate into his art.

Stein's persistently redundant sequences point up the intense energy the young artist expended in his incessant struggle to seek order and clarity in the darkness of the unknown. Using the same literary devices as above, she succeeds in devaluating his work once success had come his way. He was "clearly expressing some-thing." But what? If his work represents "something being strug-gling," and if it is viewed as an autonomous entity in the process of creation, it must alter continuously in form, shape, content, and texture as it proceeds to carve out the new. Such activity ne-cessitates struggling. Only after feelings of self-assurance and sat-isfaction have taken over does struggling cease. "Certainly every one could be certain of this thing that this one is a great one." Stein's opinions, conveyed in each of her self-contained and discontinuous sentences, point up what she considers to be the failure of Matisse's later paintings: he abandoned *struggling* and accepted fulfillment by following his "decorative" bent. Only Matisse's extraordinary colors and drawing ability carried him through. Judgmental in her approach to Matisse, Stein concludes that he failed as the harbinger of a new aesthetic.

The greater intimacy she enjoyed with Picasso allowed her more freedom to express her reactions to his art. According to Leo, the feelings of abandon implicit in her literary portrait of "Picasso" (1909) resulted from her admiration of his cubist canvases.[6] Because Stein believed instinct to be at the core of Picasso's nature, she felt he wanted to take in the whole of his vision at the outset of a work, ingurgitate it, then regurgitate it in the act of brushing forms and colors onto the canvas. In her notebooks, she remarks on Picasso's "emotional leap and courage," concluding that he *is* without question the forerunner of a new aesthetic. Traditional concepts of beauty, for example, are no longer valued in Picasso's *struggle* to flesh out new shapes. Clarity, all-important for Matisse, was not so for Picasso, nor for Stein, who, in her notebooks, made a mental note to herself: "Not express yourself like Matisse but be giving birth like Cézanne and Picasso and me."[7]

Stein marvels repeatedly in her verbal portrait of Picasso at his ever-burgeoning power to bring forth what as yet was unseen and unformulated—"something was coming out of him." She saw his work as an autonomous energetic entity in and of itself: "This one was one having something come out of him something having meaning. This one was one always having something come out of him and this thing the thing coming out of him always had real meaning." That Stein alludes many times to the verb *working* ("This one was certainly working and working.") suggests that Picasso's lifeline to the world was his work—that obsessive urge to expel the fulgurating chaos within him that, if not excreted, would kill him: "This one was one who was working and certainly this one was needing to be working so as to be one being working."

The reification of his psychological and spiritual needs are conveyed by means of adjectives suggesting weight: *heavy, solid*. Yet, the word *charming* ("one who was completely charming") lends an antithetical and superficial note to Picasso's genius, suggesting immediate accessibility. More perplexing and confusing is Stein's listing of just what was coming out of him: "a solid thing, a charming thing, a lovely thing, a perplexing thing, a disconcerting thing, a simple thing, a clear thing, a complicated thing, an interesting thing, a disturbing thing, a repellent thing, a very pretty thing."[8] Picasso's paintings from 1905–11 are, as she states above and elsewhere, both chaotic and ordered, simple and complex, clear and perplexing, pretty yet repellent.

Stein's tone, syntax, and broken rhythms convey Picasso's inner turmoil and lack of controlling logic, as well as the energy charges embedded in his canvases. Her verbal portrait is so different in tempo from the drawn-out cadences of her "Matisse."[9] Along with irregular rhythmic beats, the destruction of sequential and relational patterns of normal language give the impression of a perpetually vanishing sense of time.

Creativity is Picasso's only *logical* and continuous driving force. But it is *his* logic, *his* notion of creativity, and not that of the status quo or of Stein herself. Indeed, she sees the two of them as having something in common: just as he is instrumental in breaking the frameworks of tradition, so she dismantles the limitations imposed upon words. This and other analogies lend a different meaning and cast—even a lyrical and playful tone—to her portrait of "Picasso."

Stein's "Portrait of Mabel Dodge at the Villa Curionia" (1911) was composed when she and Toklas were visiting Dodge in Florence. Although few references are made to her hostess's estate, by her mere mention of the simplest objects, Stein generates her feelings of excitement at being there. Indeed, her technique, according to her brother, "was directly inspired by Picasso's latest [cubist] form."[10]

Stein's focus in her portrait of "Mabel" was not the woman, but rather her villa and the flavor of the environs. The "breathing" of the fresh air, the "climate," and the "garden" imbue her with "that much beginning" that "has not the same place when the ending is lessening." No noise, no distractions, but also no feelings of disappointment intrude upon that fervor she experiences. For example, the very thought of "packing" for the journey to Florence triggers all types of sensations that have a cumulative effect in the passage: the warmth of the "blankets," the "spread" on the bed, the "dress," the "expedition" and the "departure." The food, including the "raw potato," "water," the aroma within and outside the home, the household chores, the laughter and conviviality, suggest that "Nobody is alone."

Concrete images ("A plank that was dry was not disturbing the smell of burning") and abstractions ("The absence is not alternative") inject a certain element of pain experienced during her visit. Perhaps she is alluding to Toklas's jealous outburst (see chapter 1): "The particular space is not beguiling . . . and the union is won and the division is the explicit visit. There is not all of any visit."

A dancer Stein and Toklas had seen when traveling in Spain had supposedly inspired her verbal portrait of "Susie Asado" (1913). The iconographical portrait, together with its continuous puns, alliterations, repetitions, rhythms, and tonalities, lend a pleasurable and humorous note as well as a deeply sexual mood to the piece. So taken was Virgil Thomson that he wrote a piano and vocal setting for it.

The event narrated is "told" at a tea party during which such "sweet" amenities as "please" and "saids" are uttered. The dancer herself is associated with "sweet," "tea," "tray," "silver," "jelly," and "pot."

> Sweet sweet sweet sweet sweet tea.
> Susie Asado.
> Sweet sweet sweet sweet sweet tea.
> Susie Asado.

That Susie Asado is a dancer is never stated outright. A suggestion of her profession is offered in the line "A lean on the shoe this means slips slips hers." After highlighting the word *shoe,* Stein follows with a pun, "sips hers" (slippers), to depict both the object and the dancer's faulty step that may have occasioned an accident after which the artist "bobbles." Elements of her costume come into view with such words as *sash, pins,* and *crown.* The stage, decors, and lighting effects are referred to in such concretions as "sets" and "nails" that hold "trees" that "tremble" together under "ancient light grey" lending a "clean" and "yellow" golden cast to the image.

Sexuality is also alluded to during the course of the tea party in the line "Incy is short for incubus." The word *incubus* is a reference to the medieval cabalistic belief, adopted by Christianity, that an evil spirit (incubus) lies on women during their sleep and has sexual intercourse with them without their even being aware of it. Knowledge of the occurrence comes to them only through the dream. "Incy," the dancer's pet name, is also child's language for tiny, and thus does she appear on the giant stage. "Trees tremble" echo a passionate embrace, as does the "jelly" that shakes as each of the guests at the tea party dip into it.

The "old vats" in the line, "are in bobbles, bobbles which shade and shove and render clean, render clean must," allude to containers filled with liquor in an immature state, or preparations for dyeing or tanning. When warmed, their repeated up and down or bubbling movement, when assonanced with "bobbles," motions that might be made by a dancer, also bring to mind the word *bubble* as in water used for the preparation of tea or the boiling cauldron in the Witches' scene in *Macbeth:* "Double, double toil and trouble; / Fire burn and cauldron bubble" (IV, i). The "shade" may be associated with the cave in which the Witches meet and the last clause of Stein's portrait, "render clean must," evokes Lady Macbeth's obsessive hand washing in her attempt to remove her excoriating sense of guilt.

The astute concluding image, "Drink pups drink pups," is a pun on the words *drink up,* yielding a conflation of themes. So, too, is the line, "A nail is unison," hammering down and bringing together the disparate elements on stage as well as in the blending of the tea and the harmony of the guests in "Sweet sweet sweet sweet sweet tea."

"Monsieur Vollard and Cézanne" (1912) was inspired by the picture dealer's impressive book on Cézanne, which both Stein and her brother admired. As in an ideogram, Stein's sentences and phrases are vertically sequenced. The conversational tone of the portrait is reminiscent of the *poèmes conversation* made popular by Apollinaire. Stein, however, intersperses her dialogue with thoughtful and judgmental notations.

> Oh you could.
> I was pleased by a smile.
> Loud tones are smiling.
> Plain letters.
> Plain in letters.
> Sing. Sung.
> I was not occidental.

The strong opening lines imply a positive, pleasing reaction to her guest, encouraging "a smile" and joyful emotions iterated in the ebullient repetitive sounds. Fragments of conversations, segments of thought, emotions buried within a variational use of associations, observations, encounters, alliterations (*Sing. Sung*), and puns (*occidental* for *accidental*) lead to moral and aesthetic judgments revolving around *truth* and *trust*.

During Vollard's visit to Stein, the conversation was lively. The "smile" at the beginning turned into laughter after the food was eaten and the fire in the hearth had been lit, establishing an entente between the two. The visit was enjoyable. He should stay longer.

> Please me.
> By staying.
> Its pretty, its nice.
> I asked a question.
> No I'll never think of it again.
> Please do be seated.
> A watch.

The mention of a "watch" implies that Vollard has consulted his linear timepiece that regulates social life, and decides he must go. Rather than feeling bereft and empty after Vollard's departure, the picture dealer's visit has brought her fulfillment. "Yes I have gotten a new form. That isn't the word. Yes I have gotten a new form. That isn't the word."

Vollard admired Stein's literary portraits and defended them when they were attacked by critics. When, for example, one of them noted derogatorily that there "is not a single allusion" to the painter's art and that Stein "merely notes down the objects that meet her eyes," Vollard retorted: "She gives us far more than a frigid enumeration."[11]

Stein's four-line portrait of "Apollinaire" (1913), the poet known for the musicality of his verses, their caligrammatic form, puns, and colloquialisms, as well as for his pornography, his essays on cubist art, and his unhappy love affairs with Annie Playden and Marie Laurencin, is cryptic. Not only do tone and voice prevail in Stein's quatrain, but the repetition and liquidity of the *l*'s in the final line create an atmosphere of fluidity characteristic of Apollinaire's own writings. Like him, but also like Emily Dick-

inson, Stein uses homonyms (I, eye), repetitions, and alliterations
to reify her perceptions.

Such words as *pin, gas,* and *elbow,* bring to mind Apollinaire's
poem, "La Chanson du Mal-Aimé," written after his trip to London in 1903 and published in 1909. In it, he bemoans the fact
that his love, Annie Playden, has rejected him. The image of the
poet walking down the foggy and darkened London streets, his
distress sharpened by the "gas" lights ("gas strips") shining from
windows of the surrounding buildings like spots of blood on the
horizon, mirror his pain, physically (like "pin" pricks), as well as
emotionally, making him "ware" ("aware") of the great void in
his world.

Other associations come to mind in Stein's portrait, which may
also be viewed as a celebration of Apollinaire's newly published
volume of verse, *Alcools* (1913), in which "La Chanson du Mal-
Aimé" appeared. The third line, "sour stout pore, pore caesar,
pour state at," suggests a reference to the alcoholic beverage, or
spirits, which the title of Apollinaire's volume brings to mind as
well as to the banquet Picasso had given for the painter Rousseau.
It was on this occasion that Marie Laurencin, Apollinaire's lover
and a painter in her own right, imbibed too much and misbe-
haved. When rejected by her, Apollinaire's love lamentations were
conveyed in "Le Pont Mirabeau," also included in *Alcools.* Their
relationship had turned *sour,* bitter, instead of sweet, and as he
pored over his lost love in his poem, the pain felt in his *stout*
heart, once firm and determined, could no longer be contained.
Only alcohol could *pour* off the hurt. Homonymously, the French
pour, pronounced *poor,* meaning impoverished in English, indicates a distressed state, as in "pour state at." Apollinaire, usually
strong and aggressive, a pusher as in "Elbow elect," an organizer,
a "caesar," a leader, and jovial most of the time, felt, when losing
Marie Laurencin, as though he had undergone an extraction, an
evisceration, a *caesarian* section, leaving him bloodied and
bruised.

Visuality is also important in Stein's "Apollinaire": "eye lessons" are "Lessons," a significant learning step in helping him
deal with his pain. During the process, he must cut through the
protective layers of his being until he reaches that inner essence,
the "I." Only then will he succeed in transforming a blood-
soaked experience into the work of art. The homonym of *lessons*
and the French *laissons,* translated as *leave* in English, suggests

both a fascination with lessons and an equally strong desire to escape from such disciplines.

An association between "Give known" and "lessons" indicates an intake of knowledge, of life, of all that exists in the outer world. Such absorption is accomplished aggressively, with *teeth* as when biting into food and also suggests *teach,* relating to lessons, to learning, and to knowing. "Fancy teeth" brings the notion of "fantasy" to mind, from the Middle English, *fancy* and Middle French *fantasie,* reminiscent of both the intaking process and the imagination necessary for the creation of the work of art.

In *He and They, Hemingway* (1923), Stein offers her insights on the teacher/disciple relationship, the avant-garde—be it Fauvism, cubism, futurism, or surrealism, and the generation gap.

When Stein and Hemingway were introduced to each other in 1922, she was forty-eight and he, twenty-three. That she wrote her poem in a schoolchild's notebook bearing the title *The Educators of Youth* might indicate her mother/father/son feelings for him. A frontispiece featured an oval portrait of Victor Hugo and four photographs illustrating four of his most visceral works: his novels *Ninety-three* and *Notre-Dame de Paris,* his play *Lucrèce Borgia,* and his collection of poems, *Chastisements,* written when he went into exile.

The six negative anaphoras, (*Not*), from line 2 to 7, underscore Hugo's position regarding murder, for revolutionary or religious reasons, as in his novels, or crimes of passion, as in his play. His ideas on these problems also reflect those of his century: his *time.* The allusion to Hemingway's book of stories, *In Our Time,* then, is clear. So, too, may Hugo's great popularity augur well for Hemingway's literary ambitions.

In the early days of their friendship, Hemingway was Anderson's and Stein's "favorite pupil." Whereas other young writers were only "on their way," Hemingway was "to head away" or head the way. The prefix *a,* however, also suggests a decline, a movement "away" from such popularity. The repetition and puns associated with *head* and *a head,* indicate an inordinate ambition on the part of the budding writer, which seemingly is no more to her taste than are his energy, instinct, and viscerality. Like the Australian aboriginal, there is something primitive about Hemingway, preventing him at times from using his "head." He acts before he thinks, allowing instinct to prevail. She had noted this in her criticism of one of Hemingway's early short stories: his open allusion to sexual matters was *inaccrochable*. He must temper his openness and repress his needs. Like the British colonizers—"In English we know"—who knew success because they applied the thinking principle to their actions, much "to their credit," and thus succeeded in coping with "extreme savagedom."

Stein, however, preached control. Like the English settlers who dominated the Australian savages, so Hemingway, under her tutelage, must accomplish a similar feat with regard to the primitive element inhabiting his psyche. Like Hugo, also a teacher of lessons, so Stein concludes her portrait in childish and repetitive greetings of welcome and of departure, leaving the finale of her story open to conjecture.

In Stein's portrait of "Cézanne" (1923), she created a rhythmic composition based on her perception of the artist's direct relationship to the objects he depicted on his canvases and the manner in which the sensations they evoked affected her. The images, metaphors, and metonym on which her verbal composition is built are, paradoxically, fleeting episodes—nothing but the aftereffects of viewing, talking, and listening to comments on his work, experienced by her in terms of ingestion, digestion, and expulsion.

Cézanne's name and the sensations created by the objects on his canvases, either singly or sequentially, are stressed in her portrait. The referents perceived in the observer's mind's eye exist, as is usual with Stein, in the *now:* in a continuous or ongoing present. Her use of repetition—with minor variations and in a variety of contexts and time sequences—allows the *real nows* to prevail, thus revealing the subject's "bottom nature."

Stein acknowledges for gratitude to Cézanne, a "genius" who had taught her so much. Upon her arrival in Paris, she later noted in "Pictures," she knew little about art despite the fact that she had seen many canvases. "I came to Cézanne and there you were, at least there I was, not all at once but as soon as I got used to it."[12] He was also instrumental, she wrote in "Plays," in altering her traditional notions of reality; the apples and chairs she saw on a Cézanne canvas depicted "the very essence of an oil painting" inhabiting "an actual present, that is the complete actual present," and allowed it to "completely express that complete actual present."[13] Thus both Stein and Cézanne achieved anew coding and decoding of the empirical world.

Stein's "Cézanne" may be looked upon in Cézannesque fashion, as a kind of *text-object:*

The Irish lady can say, that to-day is every day. Caesar can say that every day is to-day and they say that every day is as they say.

In this way we have a place to stay and he was not met because he was settled to stay. When I said settled I mean settled to stay. When I said settled to stay I meant settled to stay Saturday. In this way a mouth is a mouth. In this way if in as a mouth if in as a mouth where, if in as a mouth where and there. Believe they have water too. Believe they have that water too and blue when you see blue, is all blue precious too, is all that that is precious too is all that and they meant to absolve you. In this way Cézanne nearly did nearly in this way Cézanne nearly did nearly did and nearly did. And was I surprised. Was I very surprised. Was I surprised. I was surprised and in that patient, are you patient when you find bees. Bees in a garden make a specialty of honey and so does honey. Honey and prayer. Honey and there. There where the grass can grow nearly four times yearly.

Stein's hermeticism does not allow readers of "Cézanne" to remain mere passive receptors of the information secreted in her lines. Nor can they, as previously suggested, proceed via external referents. Rather, they must approach Stein's verbal portrait as they would signs and symbols, thus ushering in a whole hidden realm of correspondences. The seemingly disconnected elements in "Cézanne" relate to and interlock with forms, color, planes, notions of time, and motility.

"The Irish lady," in Stein's opening clause, is a literary transliteration of a visual image. She stands unabashed by continuous conquests and by authoritarian civil rulers, that is, by the continuous present and presence of a "Caesar," dating back to Julius, the conqueror of Celtic Gaul, to the present time, when Ireland was declared a free state. Such statements refer to a virtually eternal sequence of time values that fit in perfectly with the end of the sentence, as in "to-day" and "every day." Stein's conjunction of seemingly unconnected factors, as in the above, while drawing readers away from human, temporal, and political logic, plunges them into transpersonal domains, to be experienced from a variety of expanding spatial perspectives. The seriality of the repeated assonances in the first line (lady, say, day), with their open *a* tonalities, underscores a sense of eternality as well as movement, which is voiced also in the sequentially iterated word, *day*.

The problem for the painter arises in the second paragraph, at the moment he seeks to arrest ("stay" "settled") nature's constant flux and shifting views on canvas. The mention of "a place to stay," of "settled to stay Saturday," suggests the end of the week or sabbath for Jews. This day, one of rest, is viewed as a totality, a summing up and containment of time and space in the week. Cézanne, however, failed to experience this kind of repose; he was never able to still the sound and flow of nature that filled his being, nor fix the visual images that constantly unfolded in his mind's eye. He wrote:

Here on the edge of the river, the motifs are very plentiful, the same subject seen from a different angle gives a subject for study of the highest interest and so varied that I think I could be occupied for months without changing my place, simply bending a little more to the right or left.[14]

The word *mouth*, as used by Stein, is a mimetic sign for the intake of breath (spirit) and food (physical nourishment) into the body. As the organ of speech (*logos*), the mouth is not merely to be looked upon as instrumental in the process of ingesting, but also, cognitively, as an organizing element identifiable with reason. The use of the word *mouth*, then, conveys the participation of body, mind, and spirit in the creative act and its absorption by the viewer.

The metaphor of the mouth enabled Stein's Cézanne to take nature into him, to imbibe it, and possess it. Understandably, then, Stein makes mention of water, not only implicit in the life process but as the very source of life and regeneration. As such, it represents the infinite possibilities that lie before painter and writer. As the container of all that is unformed, the germ of everything that will be, liquidity represents the potential factor in the artistic process. With more specificity, water also refers to Cézanne's canvases featuring water, such as his *Bathers*, painted in palpable liquid blues and greens or more ethereal and sublime tones.

Thus does Cézanne leap from temporal to cosmic spheres, from the waters of the earth to those of the informal heavens, thereby conflating what the empirical world reveals as separate and detached. Likewise, objects in the empirical world mirror those built into the very structure of the canvas. Although the observing eye may not discern such analogies at first, in time the interplay between the two becomes manifest; each is an active participant in the compositional quality of the work as a whole.

Stein notes her feelings of surprise ("And I was surprised") and keeps reiterating her astonishment and amazement when viewing his canvases, in reinforcement of the important role he played in her literary development. Her use of the metaphor *bee* serves perfectly to convey Cézanne's qualities and her own, as well as those of the insect—all indefatigable workers known for their organized and structured ways as they continuously busy themselves in the elaboration of a sweet viscid material from the nectar of flowers. The qualitative emphasis not only alludes to the sweetness of the honey that the bee manufactures after attaining its goal, but also to those feelings experienced by the painter and writer when achieving theirs. The diligence of the three—insects and humans—introduces a transcendent mode into the transformative process, be it in terms of the *natural* sphere of the insect or the *artificial* one of the *artist*.

"Honey and prayer" allow the creative spirit to leap from the concrete to the nonmaterial spiritual realm. In that honey, like prayer, is a primal element, it represents the sweetness of life as opposed to its bitterness. In that it flows like water in the promised land, so, too, does the sight or thought of Cézanne's canvases allow Stein to penetrate that inspirational sphere, thus making it possible for her to express her creative urge.

Stein's last line—"There where the grass can grow nearly four times yearly"—suggests the fructifying and eternally burgeoning nature of grass, a revivifying element, as were the previously mentioned water and honey. The "four," a quaternity, suggests feelings of harmony and completion effected during the creative process in general and in the presence of Cézanne's paintings in particular. Green grass, identified so frequently with Cézanne's landscapes (*Château Noir, Lake Annecy, Bend in Road at Montgéroult, Mont Sainte-Victoire,* etc.) may also be associated with Ireland, and thus the allusion to the "Irish lady" in the very first line. Ireland's emerald greenness is due to its heavy rainfall. Water, it was believed in ancient times, contained curative elements as attested to in the mythological Tuatha De Dannan's fountain (*slante*) of health. Thus is grass symbolically joined to water to become the source of life and, by extension, of creativity in general. The emerging conflation suggests to Stein a connection between text, subject, and language, which now function mimetically.

Like Cézanne, Stein found her organizational construct in her portraits, which at times were living momentos of her master's method. Like him, she divested her verbal canvases of a "frame," thus ridding herself of all hierarchies and significations. She transformed dichotomy into emphatic uniformity, and detached entities into a continuous decomposition of composition.

Chapter 4

Tender Buttons: Cubism and an Alchemical Linguistic Trajectory

Tender Buttons (1914) may be regarded as one of Stein's most innovative and most esoteric works. Like the alchemist who transmutes his metals and records his findings in iconographic representations, ciphers, and diagrams, Stein projects her continuously altering mental meanderings, meditations, visions, and free associations onto real objects, foods, and rooms. First viewed as distinct substances, the images she observes, like the chemical combinations studied by those ancient scientists, are depicted with great "exactitude."

Working with the word, rather than with the alchemists' metals, Stein's lexicon, when externalized and placed on the white sheet of paper, is explicit and redolent with clarity. Such clarity, however, is a strategy, a subterfuge, a springboard for the spawning of infinite associations and analogies.

Like the alchemists who purified the baser elements (lead) with which they worked by putting them through triturating tests, so Stein also experimented with words, requiring them to go through her version of trial by fire and water. Words that had become atrophied through centuries of use and misuse were dismembered, mutilated, stripped of their traditional and logical meanings, relationships, analogies, memories, and associations. Dross was shorn while the core, the primitive essence and melody, was retained by Stein to decant into fresh and heteroclite conjunctions of words. Such a process allowed her to receive the old word(s) in the *now*, as it had once existed long ago; in its pristine purity, dazzling, sparkling, glowing, ready for incantation in melody—in the poem.

Alchemists, who had to maintain strict secrecy concerning their experiments in order to protect themselves against persecution by the Roman Catholic Church, which believed their discoveries might in some way lessen its authority, coded their records, writing them in symbols, glyphs, and iconic signs. Stein, unwilling to reveal her most private thoughts and feelings to an unfeeling and destructive public, was likewise secretive. Accordingly, *Tender Buttons,* is a confluence of word/signs—a *mystery.*

For some, this slim volume may be looked upon as a *religious* work, but only insofar as the word *religion* is understood in its original Latin sense—Latin *religare:* to root, to bind, to link back, to reconnect with a collective past. Never, when referring to Stein, is it to be associated with organized religion. In this regard, *Tender Buttons,* divided into three parts—Objects, Food, and Rooms—may be viewed as an inner trajectory, Stein's descent into being, into the collective unconscious, the source of creation.

Painterly factors are also evident in *Tender Buttons.* Cézanne's influence, as previously noted, is primordial. As he had believed it was more important for the artist to reveal geometric structures hidden behind objects than to delineate the objects concretely, so Stein adopted a similar method with regard to the function of words. Once terms had been pared down to their essentials, the skeleton structure and bone marrow of the word and work could come forth full-blown.

Cézanne's attempt to "re-create nature" by simplifying forms, reducing them to their basic geometric equivalents, led to certain distortions, as in *Mont Sainte-Victoire* (1885–87). Likewise did Stein's signs, symbols, and glyphs appear disfigured, deformed, and because of such altered appearances, were disorienting to the viewer. Cézanne, after divesting his canvases of traditional perspective, allowed new spatial patterns to emerge, leading him to delineate objects from shifting rather than from a single point of view. The resulting interaction between flat planes, which encouraged minute transitional color tones to oscillate one against another, gave the observer the impression of vibrating surfaces. In like manner did Stein divest her words of perspective and hierarchies, endowing them, once juxtaposed, with continuous motility, and not allowing one to assume greater importance than another. Indeed, so active and vital did they become both as single and sequenced units, that she played one "lively word" against or with another in a *continuous present.*

Cézanne's views were also significant in the spawning of cubism. There were, understandably, affinities between Stein's writings, most specifically *Tender Buttons,* and the canvases of such friends as Picasso, Braque, and Gris. Like them, she emphasizes still lifes, with their commonplace objects like potatoes or asparagus, which also have their cerebral and spiritual equivalents. When embedded in the sentence, a potato or an asparagus is conveyed two-dimensionally, flatly, without adjectives; nor is memory called upon since it serves to highlight one or another element within a grammatically self-contained speech unit. Thus did Stein dispense, as had Cézanne and the cubists even more radically, with perspective and the illusion of depth. Fragmentation and dissociation of traditional literary forms and conventions allowed her the psychological and aesthetic freedom to re-create fresh verbal compositions, and in so doing, expand and implement their impact on the reader. Like the cubists also, she did not attempt to find meaning in the group of objects depicted in *Tender Buttons.* What was of import to her was the need to convey ideas and feelings relating to these forms in terms of their mass, color, texture, and line.

Stein had come a long way since *Three Lives* and *The Making of Americans* and the universal types ("bottom nature"), which she attempted to portray non-mimetically, by means of the repetitive use of verbs of being, genderless pronouns, prepositions, and conjunctions. What she now sought to capture was the *perception* of that *single moment* when the mind comes into contact with the object of its consciousness, and the sensory experience it then conveys in a continuous present. Each such occurrence is viewed by Stein as unique: no memory of a past or of a special type. Stein's mental leaps, requiring intense concentration and discipline on her part, revealed an ability to verbalize and sensorialize the effect of the shock or head-on collision between consciousness and the object of its focus in a present reality.[1]

Tender Buttons, like cubist painting, is representational. Yet, paradoxically, its gleanings are increasingly abstract and hermetic. Words used to replicate an object emerge arbitrarily. There is, then, no defining or ordering of them into readily understandable groupings. As Picasso, Braque, and Gris created their *collages,* so Stein brought forth her own pictorial reality in the word, which she viewed as a *thing* in and of itself. Unlike the cubists in their collages, she did not include fragments of newspapers, cigarette wrappers, tickets, and other sundry objects drawn from the everyday world in her writings. Her architectonic structures were built instead on polysemous words.

In *Tender Buttons*, therefore, words are for the most part non-referential, non-relational, non-ideational, non-illusionist. Devoid of descriptions and for the most part unintelligible to those whose world is limited to rational reasoning, the forward movement of Stein's lexicon is triggered by an inner necessity—by some mysterious energy. Although she did away with most of the connective signs of discourse (conjunctions, prepositions, pronouns, articles, etc.), she reintegrated the noun, the very grammatical device she had abolished in an earlier work, *The Making of Americans* (see chapter 6). Why use the superfluous? She wrote: "A noun is a name of anything, why after a thing is named write about it."[2] In time, her views changed.

And then, something happened and I began to discover the name of things, that is not discover the names but discover the things the things to see the things to look at and in so doing I had of course to name them not to give them new names but to see that I could find out how to know that they were there by their names or by replacing their names. And how was I to do so. They had their names and naturally I called them by the names they had and in doing so having begun looking at them I called them by their names with passion and that made poetry, I did not mean it to make poetry but it did, it made the Tender Buttons, and the Tender Buttons was very good poetry it made a lot more poetry.[3]

Since Stein names the thing and its qualities, but does not deal with the thing itself, her language is forcibly abstract.[4] In that concrete nouns and adjectives are linked to one another in new and what appears to be arbitrary diagrammatical order and in a variety of arrangements, with seemingly no relationship to the world of contingencies, to decipher such poetry is difficult and depends for the most part upon the depth of the reader's projection.

Although *Tender Buttons*, like the works of the ancient alchemists, is a *vas hermeticum*, let us explore associationally some poems in the collection. First, its oxymoronic title. Both qualitative and quantitative, abstract and concrete, the appeal is to the eye, the pictorial element, rather than to the ear and sound, as in her *Portraits*. The eye, identified with the archetype of consciousness, is associated with the intellect and the cognitive use of words. It has also been identified, since ancient Egyptian times, with the spirit and soul; thus does it become instrumental in creating the sacred space (*temenos*) within which the glyphs will be imprinted. In that the eye is the organ that orders, selects, and differentiates levels of reading and understanding, the aura and vibrations it experiences pave the way for its relationships with the object (or objects) depicted in the poem.

The noun *button* (from the Old French, *boton*), is a bud, sprout, shoot, tendril; *bouter* means to push, eject. It may also be associated with a knob that one pushes as on a bell, or turns to open a door; with a button on clothing; or a pimple. That Stein appends the adjective *tender* (Latin *tener*) to buttons, adds a metatextual quality to the title. Buttons, as metaphor, represent something that is growing, burgeoning; its shoots and tendrils emerging from the earth, however, are still tender and must be cared for. *Tender,* therefore, suggests something malleable, easily cut, divided, masticated, vulnerable to feeling and affection. It was Mlle. de Scudéry who, in seventeenth-century France, dreamed up the *Carte du Tendre,* representing the various paths by which one could gain access to the land of love. Isn't this exactly what interests Stein? "Poetry is doing nothing but using losing refusing and pleasing and betraying and caressing nouns."[5]

By its very ambiguity, this metatextual title has almost infinite connotations, stemming from both matriarchal and patriarchal worlds. Divested of normal order, context, function, and semantics, the associations evoked by the title, along with the poems included in the volume, have been liberated from the limitations imposed upon them by the world of contingencies. As the eye focuses on the roundness of the button, the object may be used as a meditative device, taking the reader into a space/time continuum. From this vantage point, Stein took yet another revolutionary step in her stylistic ways.

Having freed herself, as she explained in *The Geographical History of America,* from her obsession with "human nature" that she now associates with linearity and the workaday world, she has penetrated another dimension, that of the "human mind," or the transpersonal realm that one may call the collective unconscious. From this new and more detached vantage point, she succeeded in endowing common, everyday objects—dress, petticoat, etc.—with a revitalized existence, thus transforming what had been dormant or latent into something with *livingness*. Not necessarily was the object's strictly utilitarian use focused upon in *Tender Buttons;* rather, and most importantly for her, it was its essence that was revealed in the work of art. Marcel Duchamp had also expanded the simply functional nature of an object in his masterpiece *Urinal;* as had Picabia, picking out objects from the five-and-dime store, then signing his name to them, after which he labeled them works of art.

Stein's new verbal iconography, as revealed in *Tender Buttons,* transgressed the limitations imposed upon language. Disorientation resulting from her realignments of words and verbal patternings, triggered new sensations born from her humanization of the inhuman material world. Her inner trajectory, unlike Charles Baudelaire's in *The Flowers of Evil,* which was accomplished in six steps, or Dante's, in nine spheres, is undertaken in three. Segments from each level—from the world of Objects, to the domain of Food, and finally to the inner sanctum of Rooms—will be explained in terms of the writing process, sexuality, and psychology.

Step 1. Objects

Objects (Latin *objectum: jactere,* something thrown in the way of the observer), suggests anything that one sees, that affects the senses, occupies the mind, calls for attention, and sets a goal. Grammatically, objects indicate nouns or substantives that directly or indirectly receive the action of a verb; philosophically, anything that can be known or perceived by the mind. The verb, *to object,* means to oppose, expose, protest, remonstrate, expostulate, and demur. Such associations, and the many more that come to mind, suggest an intensely active, aggressive, excited, powerful, and even hostile mood on Stein's part. She seems ready to explode, to give vent, to expel her new and loving vision of language.

The fifty-eight poems included under the rubric "Objects" deal with visible, tangible, and commonplace items. Stein's asyntactical placements and alignments of words into melodic patterns and rhythms, trigger an emotional response in the reader as does a puzzle, acrostic, logograph, or anagram. In so doing, the poems titillate, frustrate, as well as bedazzle the mind.

"A Carafe, That Is a Blind Glass"

A kind in glass and a cousin, a spectacle and nothing strange a single hurt color and an arrangement in a system to pointing. All this and not ordinary, not unordered in not resembling. The difference is spreading.

The carafe—like the alchemist's crucible—is and contains mysterious elements. A bottle with a flaring lip used to hold beverages, wine, blood, or any liquid, it may be viewed in Stein's linguistic scheme as an *ideogram:* a picture, symbol, or sign used to represent a thing or an idea. No longer merely utilitarian, it has become an object of contemplation and meditation.

Pictorially, the carafe suggests the female body with its rounded, uterine-looking container at the bottom and the spreading outer lip or vagina at the top, which permits the entrance and exit of substances. Such an association is valid since Toklas moved into rue de Fleurus when Stein was composing *Tender Buttons.* It was the first time that either women had experienced a reciprocal love relationship. Unable to contain the joy of their union and fearful of revealing her sexual pleasures openly, she resorted to the ideogram to celebrate the excitement, joys, and fruitful nature of the female body.

Blind, indicating an inability to see in the outer realm, and therefore easy deception by appearances, permits on the other hand greater perception into those darkened, murky, and sometimes forbidding inner spheres. Homer, Tiresias, and Oedipus are all associated with blindness, the latter figure having gouged out his eyes in order to fathom the depth of his crimes. Were such emotions implicit in Stein's lesbian relationship? It is doubtful that she still felt guilt. Certainly, her pleasure encouraged her to intone her delight in poetry but always in a mitigated, restrained, and hermetic manner, thereby protecting herself from the aspersions of others. Was her love blind?

The description of *glass* a blind is a personification. It is opaque in its understanding of outer elements, but transparent for those who can peer inwardly, for the poet who knows how to secrete the contents of the glass. When hand blown, glass may be looked upon as an art object, worthy of admiration for its beauty, luster, color, tone—as is a beloved. If broken or chipped, as happens in relationships, the cutting, hard, and bruising edge may draw blood. The references to *glass* also suggests "spectacle"—

eyeglasses make for better sight—but also a *spectacle,* an eye-catching public or theatrical display, an object of curiosity or contempt about which one may speculate. Because of Stein's sexual proclivities and her literary objections and rebellions against staid grammatical and syntactical conventions, she was vulnerable and open, like the carafe, to public shame were she to make a "spectacle" of herself.

"A kind in glass and a cousin," suggests a qualitative relationship, rooted in kindness and understanding. It may also intimate a type of bond to which a relative may be kindly disposed, though such a "spectacle" might lead some "to pointing" their finger at the object of their ire, thus casting opprobrium on the couple in question, despite the fact that there is "nothing strange" about such "an arrangement" or "system." Singly or individually, people "hurt" others for any reason at all—a different literary "system" or unusual sexual proclivities. In so doing, they draw blood ("color"), the "color," referring to wine contained in the carafe, which brings merriment, or as in communion, commemorates a bond or sacrament, thus uniting what had been divided and transforming the temporal into the atemporal. "A single hurt color" implies the pain of blood issuing from a cut or from menstruation, mirroring the bruising lot of women who are looked down upon in a patriarchal "system." Yet, this very liquid contained in the carafe/uterus is the sine qua non of life, that which permits its continuation. Redness, which intimates embarrassment and "not ordinary" passion is catalytic, but "not unordered," dissimilar "in not resembling" the behavior of the majority. While "The difference" between Stein's way as a lesbian poet and society may be increasing or "spreading," this sentence also refers to the lips of the vagina/carafe that, when opened up, allow the mysteries hidden within its liquid body to be decanted.

"Glazed Glitter"

Although a mood of jubilation and excitement also prevails in "Glazed Glitter," a warning is offered to those who take the world of appearances at face value:

Nickel, what is nickel, it is originally rid of a cover.
The change in that is that red weakens an hour. The change has come.
There is no search. But there is, there is that hope and that interpretation

and sometime, surely any is unwelcome, sometime there is breath and there will be a sinecure and charming very charming is that clean and cleansing. Certainly glittering is handsome and convincing.

There is no gratitude in mercy and in medicine. There can be breakages in Japanese. That is no programme. That is no color chosen. It was chosen yesterday, that showed spitting and perhaps washing and polishing. It certainly showed no obligation and perhaps if borrowing is not natural there is some use in giving.

The alliteration in the poem's title, "Glazed Glitter," and the previous poem's "Glass," suggests an object with a mirrorlike, sparkling, glossy, and highly polished surface. Although hard and immobile, like fired clay or enamel, its bedazzling, scintillating, flickering, and rippling exterior infuse it with life and dynamism. Let us recall that alchemists used *nickel*, a silvery hard ductile metallic element capable of a high polish and resistance to corrosion, in their scientific transmutations. Because of its gray/silvery tones, it was likened to lead, a base or unrefined metal, identified by alchemists with Saturn, the God of Time, and thus of death. The German *kupfer* (nickel), deceptively labeled copper, accounts for the "red" in the second sentence, perhaps referring to the moon, thus symbolizing change when identified with the woman's monthly menses. With the flow of time, the once-brilliant coloration "weakens an hour," growing paler and more feeble with each passing moment.

"The change in that is that red weakens an hour," indicates flux and aging as well as the desire to be forthright and open, to be "rid of a cover." In that nickel is also change (five-cent piece) that passes from hand to hand, it is a common denominator, facilitating commercial transactions in the everyday world. So should the word and its object be plain and commonplace. "The change has come" implies a change in time but also of monetary values, referring perhaps to Stein's financial transactions with her brother. Their once-glittering and bedazzling works of art, food for spirit and soul, had, when sold, taken on functional value. A question of tender, they now resemble the impure and leaden metals rather than the solely golden and aesthetic ones. "There is no search" now for higher worth—that of eternal values in art. Yet, there is "hope" in the "interpretation" and aftermath of such a transaction, though "sometimes, surely any is welcome." The mention of "breath" (*pneuma*), a sublimating force, refers to spiritual and creative powers within a being; others see it as a "sinecure" to be viewed as a disease, *sine cure,* that is, without a cure. Idleness is "charming," as Leo and Stein knew only too well. Relationships change, however; emotions and passions have a "cleansing" factor; they "clean" away the rubble, the dross, allowing for the essence of kinship to emerge: "Certainly glittering is handsome and convincing."

That "There is no gratitude in mercy and in medicine," intimates Stein's loss of expectation in science, relying more deeply at present on feelings as her guide. The "breakages in Japanese" may refer to Leo's collection of Japanese prints, also broken up during the division, thus mirroring the shattering of the brother/sister friendship. It was not so intended; there was "no programme" for such a happening. Nor was choice involved. Things had to be cleared up: anger, which "showed spitting," also viewed as a cleansing process for Orientals, reinforces Stein's frequent use of "washing and polishing," cleansing and cleaning. Nor was there any "obligation" that she share her life/art with her brother; no "borrowing," henceforth, between them. Her anger has dissipated. The need to be generous is uppermost now, "yet may there be some use in giving."

Stein seems to have traversed her Rubicon. The "glazed glitter" that prevails since Toklas moved to 27, rue de Fleurus, brightening, cleaning, and cleansing her life, bringing to it unheard of beauty, polish, and glitter, thus extracts the silvery and reddened tones from the object/life. The matriarchate had taken full sway over the partriarchate with its "handsome and convincing" autocracy of monetary values.

"A Box"

In "A Box," viewed as a feminine symbol because of its containing/uteruslike quality, may also be identified with the cranium, the home of secret, fragile, precious, but also fearful elements. Protective as well as imprisoning, the brain case is the seat of potentiality, the origin of infinite riches, but also of distress, disease, and all of life's iniquities. Yet, as in Pandora's box, there is hope. When identified with a coffin, as in Osiris' case, the box symbolizes decay that, in alchemical view, is the locus for transformation from unregenerate to productive matter.

What emerges from within Stein's box? Ideas, feelings, sensations revolving around a human body? a brain? Qualitative factors, implicit in the poems already analyzed, reappear: "kindness," for example, may be so unexpected for some as to elicit "redness" or blushing; "rudeness," may provoke the "redness" of rage. The "rapid" barrage involving the "same question" also provokes anger, redness, and rudeness. The "eye," the organ of enlightenment and perception, probes the emotions that surge forth. Its careful "research" and "selection," painful at times, eliminates the "cattle" or multiple riches that exist within the box/cranium and the box/body. "Cattle" may also suggest domestication: these animals, considered property, are raised for the masses, that is, society's lowest common denominator. "Cattle" are like the commonest of objects Stein uses in her ideograms and cubists in their paintings. She succeeds in creating a work of art by her discerning placement of these objects in her poem, thus altering both their meaning and focus. A writer, like a cook who cleans food by stripping it of its dross, must peer critically into everything that emanates from his box/cranium and box/body: idea, emotion, sensation. The conscious mind must control, edit, classify each single moment of experience. Never should emotions be allowed entry into the written work without having first been probed and purified by the eagle "eye." The first syllable of "Question," indicates a *quest*, a search, thus underscoring the mental operation of "selection," the notion of looking, finding, seeking, spying, thereby separating the wheat from the chaff. The multiple alliterations, (*r, s, c, s, q, p*), underscoring sibilants, labials, gutturals, palatals, sound out the intense struggle existing within the *box:* "rudimentary" contents within the unconscious, which seek so desperately to surface.

What does "order" outside of the box, that is, in the world, imply? What is the "white" (Steinese baby talk for right) "way" for the "cattle" to take themselves or be taken out of the pasture? The virgins, referring to traditional values concerning the body and mind, like "cattle" do not like to be led out of their secure and contented ways. Enclosed within the pasture, however, virginal views "disappoint" both the thinking and sexually active person. So, too, is it easier for the writer to adhere to conventional ways (imitate the nineteenth-century techniques) and for the virgin to experience the normal (heterosexual) act of intercourse, "suggesting a pin" rather than to try the different (lesbian) way. The world outside of the boxed-in world may disorient, one may lose one's way and go "round" in circles, thus paving the way for a visionless, nondifferentiated, intellectually and sexually blinding life. Cut off from dangers, one is also severed from the excitement engendered by "a fine substance strangely." Withdrawal encourages vulnerability to hurt, but also to pleasure of the most "rudimentary" kind. Reactions, therefore, must "be analysed," cognized, contemplated, sifted, pruned. The discovery of "strangely" delicate, subtle, sensitive elements within being are to be pinpointed. All factors in the life process are invited to be scrutinized: the "green point," suggesting fertility; the "red," implying pain and menstruation. Each factor must serve to transform what remains latent and dormant within the "box" into active forces, be it in the domain of art or in human relationships.

"Petticoat"

Although not an overt subscriber to feminism, Stein, in her one-line poem, "A Petticoat," clearly displays her ire against the patriarchal Judeo-Christian society with its hierarchy of unsavory and deficient values. While emphasizing the fine dividing line between acceptable ways—the pure, virginal "light" and "white"—as opposed to the usually black "ink spot," she is referring to the writer who strays from conventional ways and is considered a "disgrace" to society. The spot left from "menstruation," viewed as unclean, symbolizes a rejection of women. Yet, both have their "rosy charm." Who better than Stein understood the meaning of "disgrace"? Her writings had been refused by so many publishers, her ideas and behavior discredited. She was an outcast. Yet, even in pain, straying out of the "pasture" held its "rosy charm" for the writer and the woman.

"Peeled Pencil. Coke" and "This Is This Dress, Aider" are two essentially pornographic poems. The first consists of three words, "Rub her coke." An example of Stein's stripping of phonemes down to their bare essentials, the alliterated title, "Peeled Pencil," suggests another kind of fruitful defloration: the readying of the vagina for the insertion of the dildo. The creative process is implicit in the phallic symbol of the pencil: as used by the poet, this instrument serves to make its mark on the paper. In the old days, pencils had to be peeled to be sharpened. As layer upon layer was being pulled off, its slender black cylinder essence was made ready to "pin" point the author's glyphs on the virginal page. Like the sexual, so the writing process arouses passion. Excitement reaches such a pitch that some feel as if their windpipe had been blocked, causing near strangulation.

To Rub, an active verb, defined as subjecting to back and forth or circular action with pressure and friction, as in cleaning, polishing, and smoothing, also suggests the hand massaging the surface of the body, thus generating friction and heat. The writer likewise encounters difficulties as she moves her hand across the page in an effort to smooth and polish the words in the manuscript. So, in alchemy, after the flammable, volcanic, ebullient powers have surged forth, distillation must take place. "Coke," the residue of coal and used as fuel, is what remains following the burning, triturating, or cleansing operation. In Stein's poem, "coke" symbolizes the transformatory round that must take place for the quintessential experience (the poem or sexual act) to make its mark on body, psyche, and intellect. Only after the raw or primitive experience has been lived can "coke" be extracted: that active substance that fuels both the sexual and creative process. "Coke," short for cocaine, acts as a local anesthetic and induces intoxication as well—something Stein never abided. Lucidity was her guide. Rather than "Coke," implying cock and coitus, she uses cunnilingus for sexual fulfillment.

"This Is This Dress, Aider"

In "This Is This Dress, Aider," Stein not only decorticates her words of conventional meaning, but uses, as always, onomatopeias and multiple puns to strengthen the point she is trying to make. The noun *Dress*, an outer garment that serves to hide the body, used as a verb, depicts the act of covering, hiding, secreting—a sexually exciting thought. Like a fetish, the dress as object is endowed with its own energy and magical qualities, thus transmuting the image into a tantalizing power. A feeling of "distress" (*this dress*) counters the joyous mood of anticipation, opening up the writer to the fear and frustration arising from her partner's built-in inhibitions, which prevent sexual fulfillment.

Aider why aider why whow, whow stop touch, aider whow, aider stop the muncher, muncher, munchers.

A jack in kill her, a jack in, makes a meadowed king, makes a to let.

"Aider," is Alice, the active participant in this poem. Like ei-
derdown, her presence is soft, pliable, and comforting. It is she
who comes to the poet's *aid* and *aids her*. As the poet's scientific
and medical side ponders the question as to "why" rapture takes
place during coitus, she realizes that for highs to reach their peak,
intellectuality must be stripped. To yield fully to instinct and to
feeling, to basic or primitive elements, allows her to go beyond
the state of reason and self-control. Rapturously and repeatedly,
she expresses her glee: "whow whow stop touch, aider whow,
aider stop." No longer is voice subverted; on the contrary, it is
allowed to sing out the overwhelming, almost trancelike state she
now experiences. The word *muncher,* someone who chews with
relish, is an onomatopeia, its nasals and fricatives suggesting the
action involved in oral sex and the sonorities accompanying such
labial activities.

Fairy tales about Jack the Giant Killer, Jack and the Beanstalk,
Jack Sprat, Jack-in-the-box, and many more, although frightening
and humorous to children and adults, also trigger the imagination. So the writer's fantasy world is likewise aroused by the
thought of sexual play, and the sensations evoked *aid* her in finding the word that will replicate the experience. A *jack,* is also a
mechanical and portable device for exerting pressure or lifting a
heavy body a short distance. The emphasis on this twice-
mentioned "a jack in" recalls a similar heaving or hoisting motion in Stein's later "Lifting Belly," referring in both cases to the
use of the dildo to bring on a climax. The word *meadowed,* associated with a tract of moist low-lying grassland, may be a metaphor for pubic hair. "King," ruler, master, and center of all he
surveys, suggests the male partner—in this case, Stein, who always considered herself man, potentate, supreme consciousness,
and creative principle, while Toklas was the woman, the home-
body, and subservient in every way.

Step 2. Food

Stein's second step in her initiatic journey into the wonder-
working elements of nature and of language, deals with food.
Fuel for the body/mind, such nourishment as is mentioned in the
fifty-one poems included in this section represents Mother Nature
as both vital and destructive. The giver of life and energy, she sees

to the propagation of the vegetal and animal worlds with which Stein now deals. Such a focalization suggests a need to regress to a primitive mode: the nonhuman psyche, the instinctual domain, in order to root out the very substance of word and sexual experience. Stein's desire to deal with common everyday entities such as foods replicates a similar movement on the part of the writer to "flatten out" poetic themes, as Arthur Rimbaud and Jules Laforgue had accomplished before her. In order to succeed, the writer must immerse herself in primal waters and bathe in the very source of existence. Only then can such vital questions as life and death be posed. These notions had always haunted Stein. Now, for the first time, they would no longer be posed from an intellectual, scientific, or philosophical point of view, but viscerally, via Mother Nature's fertility rites.

For the alchemist, food was energy—that is, the fire or catalyst needed to perform the operation that transmuted base metal into sublime gold. To effect such a change was arduous and painful, requiring the burning and water operations that stripped and cleansed the problem, thus isolating it from other elements. Stein's poetic needs may be examined similarly. Her intense search in the domain of language took her from the outer world, "the glazed glitter," into the very heart of physical being. Her trajectory, she believed, had helped her better assess her needs and her worth, thus aiding in the transmuting of feeling into its authentic container, the *word*.

Food also has a qualitative factor appended to it. Identified with agressivity, it is the mouth's task first to take it from the outside world, then masticate ("muncher"), ingest, digest, and finally eliminate it. So, too, must the word be internalized, experienced, sensed, palpated, prior to its implantation into the poem. Life and the creative process, then, require a combative, invasive, and militant stance.

"Milk"

A symbol for abundance and fertility, milk is nature's sustaining force par excellence. For mystics, such as the Orphics, it spells immortality; for the Druids, it was used for curative purposes. The inconographic representations of Isis, Hera, and Mary nursing their young, represent Mother Nature in her most fructifying form. The *Philosophical Stone* (Spiritual God), the summation of the alchemical operation, was referred to as "Virgin's Milk," for it brought immortality.

Climb up in sight climb in the whole utter needles and a guess a whole guess is hanging. Hanging hanging.

The vertical act of climbing to the breast or "utter" (udder) to suck out the fluid of life—a natural act for infants—requires effort, exertion, striving. Stein's verbal portrait, "Picasso" comes to mind: her admiration for his valiant and continuous struggle in contrast to "Matisse" who, once fame was his, abandoned the battle and renounced the challenge. Be it in the artistic or love process, contention is crucial; passivity, lethargy, an inability to concentrate and focus on one's goal, is death.

The word *utter,* closely allied in Stein's punning ways to a cow's udder, conflates the intellectual and the physical worlds. Without such sucking activity, the physical energy needed in the practical as well as the poetic worlds would be wanting. That the cow image is implicit in utter/udder is not, in Stein's view, a derogatory epithet attached to womankind. On the contrary, having recourse to it in many of her writings, she uses it to symbolize the nourishing aspect of Mother Earth.

"Needles," used repeatedly in the first section of Stein's work, are phallic images, suggesting pain during the act of penetration. In that they are also employed in sewing, designed to bind together bits of disparate cloth, they fuse the heteroclite. Likewise, the word is interwoven or intertwined into the text. To needle someone is to annoy, upset; but the energy aroused in such activity is catalytic. It is worth recalling that the cubists stuck pins and nails into their collages, introducing a non-painterly element onto the canvases, thus rejecting while also expanding the prevailing logocentric definition of art. Nor are Stein's texts devoid of such puncturing and piercing objects. Hurt necessarily plays a role in the creative process as well as in human relationships.

"A guess a whole guess is hanging" implies the world of the unknown that comes into being as the milk of life is suckled. Nor are the sexual pleasures derived from such an act to be overlooked by the sensualist that Stein was. *Guess* (from Middle English *gessen*) suggests *get,* which like *Climb,* allows for the fulfillment of the wishing, wanting, and needing. The food (omitting the g leaves *essen,* to eat in German) within the "hanging" breast endows the one who "climbs" with energy, to be expended in sexual, philosophical, or literary activity. Within milk/breast exists the potential for life; within it *hangs* the fate of the human (intellect) and animal (body) species.

"Hanging hanging" is a reference to breasts in general and, in particular, Stein's pendulous ones. Within them resides the unknown, the unforeseen—that creative power that makes her world go round. Metaphors for security, tenderness, intimacy, breasts are an offering as well as a refuge.

"Potatoes"

Stein's three poems dealing with potatoes, a spherical, bulbous root nourished within the heart of Mother Earth, visualize the notion of growth and creativity. That the French equivalent for potato, *pomme de terre,* or apple of the earth, is the terrestrial counterpart of paradise's forbidden fruit that hangs from the tree of knowledge, conflates what had been severed according to Genesis. Unlike the spiritual fruit that leads to transgression, the *potato* yields knowledge of another sort: it permits an ingestion of earthly and everyday matter, thus serving to fructify both mind and body. Existential, the potato symbolizes this present life—the *now*—rather than the Christian's view of future heavenly domain.

POTATOES "Real potatoes cut in between."
POTATOES "In the preparation of cheese, in the preparation of crackers, in the preparation of butter, in it."
ROAST POTATOES "Roast potatoes for."

The three poems focus on the preparation of potatoes: from the raw and cutting phase, the cooking operation, to its final state in the serving.

The image in the first poem, reminiscent of Georgia O'Keefe's many opening or severed flowers, replicates the dividing and severing process in making the potato ready for eating. The cutting open of the vegetable opens up its secret parts to the light of the eye. So, too, may the "cut in between" be applied to other areas, needing no profound decoding since its message is more than obvious. In terms of the poet, however, to articulate requires a cutting up, a trimming and slimming of syllables in the preparation of the word's implantation into the text.

That "cheese" and "butter" in the second poem are added in the cooking process not only increases the vegetable's succulence, but in that they are milk products, they increase its nutritive powers. So, too, must the poet include foreign materials, as had the cubists, to enrich a text. "Crackers" are not only a dry crispy bread product made of leavened or unleavened bread used to mop up the delectable sauce from a dish or platter, but they also make snapping or crackling noises. To the combination of potatoes, cheese, and butter, a feast for the taste buds, is added the agreeable crackling sonorities from the "crackers" being eaten, but also those emanating from the oven as the "roast" (referred to in the third poem) is cooking, thus also becoming food for the ear. *Crackers* broken down into *crack-er* (her), has a sexual allusion, referring back to "the cut in between" in the first poem; and to the effort made by the poet, cracking her brain to come out with the proper combination of words to be added during the cooking process.

"Asparagus"

That a fat and ungainly woman is alluded to as a sack of potatoes, an image that can readily be applied to Stein, may help to explain the poem entitled "Asparagus," referring, perhaps to Toklas's thinness.

Asparagus in a lean in a lean to hot. This makes it art and it is wet wet weather wet weather wet.

Asparagus, (Greek *spargan*) meaning to swell, is iconographically tall and pencil-like, and thus a phallic symbol. A perennial plant of the lily family having many-branched stems and minute scalelike leaves, the asparagus is cultivated for its edible shoots. No longer dealing with an invisible and secret world with regard to the potato, Stein broaches an ocular and delectable one. That the object depicted is "lean" suggests skinniness, but also the act of inclining, bending, or casting one's weight to one side for support. In these cases, it alludes to Toklas: her skeletal appearance, her subservience, her bending and fawning when in the presence of her deity; also the awkwardness of the sexual position when making love to Stein. The "hot" refers to the heat brought on by the rubbing operation during the sexual encounter; the "wet

wet weather," to the perspiration resulting from such friction; and "wet weather wet," to the vaginal fluids discharged preceding and following the climax. There may also be a literary allusion: the efforts expended by Stein as she leans first on one word or artistic form and then another. The intensity poured into the choices she must make in the writing process generates bodily heat, liquidity, and when completed, moments of Dionysian ecstasy.

"Chicken"

Stein's many poems dealing with meats (roast beef, mutton, sausages, chicken) take us into the animal world, antithetical to Platonists and Christians who prize spirituality rather than instinctuality. Not so for Stein who loved animals, and especially dogs. In keeping with Western values, to allude to the animal in an individual is to refer to what is base or, in alchemical terms, is leaden and unrefined in that person. Yet, it is the animal as *libido*, raw energy, that empowers creation.

The "Chicken," the title Stein gave to four poems, is a barnyard animal, not too clean, not too bright, and easily scared. It may also refer to the coward, the young woman as a term of endearment, or to a prostitute, as well as to the young male homosexual.

The "Pheasant," unlike the common chicken, is a sought-after game bird known for its long sweeping tail and brilliant feathers. On the other hand, the chicken is "a peculiar bird," different, curious, odd, known for its eccentricities. Used in some religious, initiatory, and divinatory rites by shamans, the chicken symbolizes death and resurrection. In Orphic rituals, it is associated with the dog, friendly to humans. According to the ancient Egyptians and Greeks, the chicken leads the dead to the lower worlds—psychologically, to inner (unconscious) realms.

That Stein emphasizes the words *dirty* and *third* intimates an association between Christianity's (Trinity) view of dirt and women (the chicken is identified with the female). The emphasis placed by revealed religions on purity and virginity was anathema to Stein, as was their view of dirt as being synonymous with evil. Dirt and evil are implicit in the world of differentiation, thus of earthly existence. To reject these aspects of life is to seek to escape into the pristine purity of an afterlife, without ever knowing terrestrial joy. The same may be said of the writer's approach to his art. For Stein, all themes, all words, from the most commonplace to the most ethereal, fueled her pen providing they were picked, prepared, and served on the proper platter.

Like a collage, cooking and writing require the introduction of other ("more") foods into the dinner or completed text. Various plants in the mustard family, like "Cress," add a pungent flavor to the meat; as do "Potato" and "Loaves" of bread. The combination of foods and seasoning, like that of letters in a word or morphemes in a text, enhance the visual beauty of the arrangement on the platter as well as its aroma and taste during its ingestion.

As previously noted, eating is an aggressive act that in the case of the pheasant and chicken begins with the catching, continues with the killing of the bird (sticking), and then the depluming (sticking), cleansing of the inside ("sticking"); and then the "sticking" of it into the mouth, masticating, pulverising, digesting it. The repetition of *stick,* its strident sibilants, hostile dentals, grating gutturals, and ferocious fricatives, stick the ear with a medley of unpleasant cacophonies, thus replicating the murderous intent of the eater. This same analogy may be applied to sexuality, for example, during a sadistic act, with all of the "extra" "sticking" devices needed to bring on the climax. Nor should the writer be discouraged from entering into verbal sadomasochistic play, in the annexing, rejecting, and redefining of terms. For everything, positive and negative, must participate in the feast that is writing.

Stein has taken the *mystery* of matter from the world of objects to that of plants and animals. Her third step will deal with the inner sanctum, viewed in terms of body and mind (both conscious and unconscious). Like the alchemist working in silence in his laboratory, so the verbal draftsman fashions, shapes, colors, and texturizes his words, clauses, sentences, and paragraphs. The labors in both cases are conducted in the secret realms of remote climes.

Step 3. Rooms

The heart of the transformatory process takes place in the room/chamber/cavern. In ancient Egypt, initiates entered the most secret vaults within the pyramid to undergo their initiatory rituals: the transformation of the potential or unformed into the fulfilled and formed. Such a conversion was looked upon as a death of the old self and the birth of the new, purified, and elevated one.

The room in *Tender Buttons* represents that solitary area within the psyche into which libido (energy) withdraws in order to revitalize what has become worn and arid within being. Comparable to the womb, where the seed is nourished, or the vaginal area where the climax may be experienced, or the mind, replete with ideas, the room provides the seclusion and separation from the outside world that is crucial to the evolution of an individual.

Withdrawing into an inner space permits Stein to cut herself off from the excitement of the workaday world that drains and deletes her energies. Within the peace and security of her own mind/room, or vaulted cranium, Stein is able to sense and think authentically. Thus does she feel able to transmute the fruit of her meditations into the word. Within the mind (conscious and unconscious spheres) she learns to see, hear, listen, and palpate in a space/time continuum; thus does she feel competent to reorganize volume, space, and form, and all other inconstants. No limitations are imposed upon the senses, now reactivated by the inflow of energy into the psyche.

The tangled terminology and rescrambling of ideas and notions occurring in "Rooms," no longer made up of separate poems, but divided into paragraphs, is as esoteric, perhaps even more so, than the previous sections. No better paradigm of Stein's ambiguous views can be offered than her repeated use of *centre*. She warns ("Act so that there is no use in a centre") against imprisonment within a rationally conceived *centre:* that is, within concepts. According to Cézanne's vision of composition, the painter's and the writer's goal is to portray each object and all of its parts in positions that are equally responsive to his sensibility and to the livingness of his observation. All hierarchies within the frame, as well as the frame itself, are abolished. The center, therefore, is no longer the center of focus of anything; nor is it to be regarded as an organizing principle.[6] No frame; no point of reference; no boundaries. A poem has no more a center than does a canvas. The cubists' dictum is: an "object is an object"; its place in the composition is "decentralized"; its ideations and iconography are transformed into the object of the composition.

The same is true of the *centre* in "Rooms" if viewed three-dimensionally, that is, as the focalizing point on a classical com-

positional canvas or the suspenseful line in a poem or novel.
When viewed four-dimensionally, however, as in such age-old religious symbolic images as the Star of David, Cross, Circle, and so
on, the *centre* is everywhere and nowhere. Some mystics refer to
this transpersonal *centre* existing within a space/time continuum
as the Principle, Absolute, or God. Pascal, quoting Hermes Tris-
megistus, wrote, "God is a sphere the center of which is everywhere and the circumference nowhere." Stein, the nonbeliever, as
God/the artist, must reach the creative center living inchoate and
transpersonally within her. In this most sacred and unknowable
region exists the beginning and end of all things in an eternal
now. Forever spawning and disintegrating, life exists as a continuously reshuffling, redirecting, rebalancing, and rekindling
process.

If the centre has the place then there is distribution. That is natural.
There is a contradiction and naturally returning there comes to be both
sides and the centre. That can be seen from the description.

Active and dynamic, the writer who plunges into a continuously shifting, expanding, and unlimited inner space, know *chaos*
(the *void*). As conveyed in Genesis and in many creation myths,
including Hesiod's *Theogony,* such fomenting mass yields, paradoxically, new insights while concomitantly dismantling non-
functioning ones. Words, when inhabiting this dark, moist, and
unlimited realm, expand in meaning, sensation, texture, and coloration. As their consistencies alter, so does their impacting upon
other phonemes and morphemes in the sentence. Although word
is one, it is made up of individual letters, each possessing its own
identity, confluence, sensation, rhythms, and blendings, thus act-
ing and reacting on the rest "of the herd" as the poet Stéphane
Mallarmé used to say.

Body, psyche, and mind are energized by Stein's intuitive forays
into and out of her *centre.* A redistribution in the placement of
words in the sentence detaches them from conventional use, thus
redefining them and pushing them to the extreme limit of language. Because of Stein's paratactical intervals, aided and abetted
by her omission of punctuation, subjects, and objects, and the addition of a plethora of puns, extreme syntactical distortion and
incomprehensibility are the result.

Metaphors, analogies, and associations to the pleasure and pain involved in the sexual and literary acts, for example, pepper the entire text: *stress, distress, pain, joy, accomplishing, lifting, voice, centre, spreading, black line, distribution, kneeling, opening, rubbing, erection, swelling, open, four, startling, starving, husband, betrothed, sleeping, size, torn, sack, hangings, movement, bed, disorder, funnel, cape, conundrum, torn, target, breath, window, milk, water, empty, flower, cutting, clean, pecking, petting, asparagus, fountain,* and so forth.

Coitus is alluded to in and of itself, but also its effect on mind and body is also suggested. The tremulous sensations triggered by climaxes and the sensual excitement generated, activates the poetic process. Described as an alchemical operation, Stein writes: "Burnt and behind and lifting a temporary stone and lifting more than a drawer."

The fire of passion produced during the sexual act heightens the flame or electric spark, which in turn, and in keeping with the alchemical process, not only burns off impurities, but dries out all moisture. Only "burnt" or charred remains are left "behind" (posterior), that is, the word's quintessence. Like a precious diamond, the word is no longer embedded in black carbon, but is polished, glittering, and gleaming with incandescent emotions, now that the old and unproductive perceptions and sensations have been killed.

The reborn and recrystallized insights are "lifting" (sexually and creatively) the poet into new areas of feeling and of expression. The "stone" that was raised suggests the removal of a veil: inhibitions have been dropped, adding to the impetus of the electric charge. An androgynous element, stone constitutes the wholeness and fullness of the primordial state, which has now been made accessible. But the experience of the sexual and verbal act, like unrefined and unshaped "stone," must be smoothed and polished, thus fulfilling its goal—the transformation of brute matter into the work of art. "Drawer," a boxlike entity used for storage, may be opened or closed. In like manner, ideas and feelings may be covertly or overtly conveyed in a poem. Stein's use of the comparison *more* suggests her increasing self-confidence in her talent as a writer.

Sight, always crucial for Stein, be it in her observation of paintings or words, is explicit in the following sentence:

No eye-glasses are rotten, no window is useless and yet if air will not come in there is a speech ready, there always is and there is no dimness, not a bit of it.

Within the secret space that is the room, the use of such devices as "eye-glasses" not only enhance vision, but protect the eye from the dirt outside. Since the "window" for Plato represents an opening onto the soul, such apertures increase the reception of Light from the spirit, senses, and mind on a variety of levels. Thus, every "window" serves the poet. Like eyeglasses, the "window," inviting air (spirit) to permeate formerly enclosed quarters, expands horizons. The eye/window may now indulge in a dual activity: to look *out* onto the world and *within*, into the deepest recesses of the *room:* body, psyche, soul. The world, like all other concrete or abstract notions, alters in meaning, consistency, texture, and coloration depending upon the light shed on it during the observing process. Such a seeing and looking activity is crucial. Such voyeurism helps her convey the carnality of language in social discourse.

"Air," a sublimated element, suggests height, spirituality, flight, an amorphous condition rather than the previously solid material principle. Such alteration of focus implies spiritual growth, an ability to abstract and conceptualize problems by divesting them of earthly entanglements. Air may be identified with "breath" (Hebrew *ruh*), the spirit of God as it moved over primordial waters in the beginning of time and created the world (Gen. 1:2). With breath, according to Judeo-Christian and Hindu belief, came the word and speech (John 1:1; Rig-Veda 1:164). Those who can see into matter and spirit sense the word; for them "there always is and there is no dimness, not a bit of it."

In another entry, Stein writes: "The time when there is not the question is only seen when there is a shower. Any little thing is water." Experienced as transpersonal and immanent, *time,* like the creative instinct, is both temporal and atemporal. As for the word imprinted on the page and embedded in matter, it too becomes abstracted, as thought. *Question* (from the Latin, *quaestio*), identified with *quest* (Latin *quaestus*), indicates a continuous search or process leading to fulfillment. The spirit of interrogation, so crucial to the writer, vanishes when the sensate world submerges the rational sphere. Yet, it has its positive attributes. Like the Flood, a "shower," identified with emotion, inundates.

On the other hand, for the alchemist and poet, the water operation both solves and dissolves. In so doing, the unsolvable problem vanishes. What had been a stumbling block has been liquefied, as sugar or salt when placed in a bowl of water. A smoother or more objective and comprehensive attitude may therefore come into being. Problems, now viewed in particles, may be divided, thereby altering perspectives and approaches to them. The particular, rather than the whole, comes under scrutiny. If, however, currents are too swift, the "shower" leads to drowning, regression, and loss of identity. "Any little thing is water" suggests that rigid, fixated, and solidified attitudes and their accompanying words may be turned into a solution—that is, be allowed to flow freely. The poet, then, is given the freedom to evaluate and reevaluate, to position and reposition them, thus bringing a new reality into being.

There is no end to the meanings and interpretations one may glean on reading *Tender Buttons*. Each word imprinted on the page may trigger in the reader ideas, melodies, rhythms, colorations, codes, and the infinite reverberations to which these give rise. Stein's inner journey or descent into the mystic's *centre,* as conveyed in *Tender Buttons,* was a breakthrough—a turning point in her life as woman and writer. Successful in subverting the Westerner's logic and habitual modes of rumination, always anathema to her, she discovered her own working order. First visualizing her object, she then interiorized it by way of the cooking operation, through which she assimilated its energy. Finally, like the good alchemist she was, she sublimated and abstracted its contents, after which it was ready to be embedded in the text. Her bristling treatment of discourse and syntax, her polysemous meanings and meanderings, her subvocal nonsense, and her verbal and ideational fragmentations were spectacular examples of what could be called the cubist language.

As cubist and alchemist, Stein, the word stripper, offers her bewitching, puzzling, and frustrating brew to contemporary readers. May each and every one plunge into its infinite waters.

5

xxxxxxxxxxxxxxxxxxxxxxxxxxxxxxxxxxxxxxxxxxxxxxxxxxxxxxxxxxxxxxxxxxxx

Theater and Opera: Static Dynamism in the Noneventful Moment

Were Steinian theater and opera really ground breaking? Were there precedents for her noneventful, non-mimetic stage works? What specifically was the nature of her innovations?

Steinian theater did have precedents. Alfred Jarry's *King Ubu* (1896), with its intentionally childish deceits, its militantly antirealistic bent, its wooden, puppetlike creatures whose voices sounded a "special" monochord and detached tone, created a virtual riot on opening night. His blatant rejection of traditional theater inspired such disciples as Guillaume Apollinaire, proponent of nonobjective painting, and a friend of Stein's, to operate upon reality as he saw fit in his excitingly different *The Breasts of Tiresias*, begun in 1903 and completed in 1917. Apollinaire's antimimetic stagecraft featured a talking kiosk that also sang and even danced; the play's capricious lines, nonrelated scenes, seemingly nonsensical songs, featured a reality beyond the world of appearances. Another of Stein's friends, Jean Cocteau, wrote stage works devoid of the characteristics of the well-made, psychologically oriented drama with its evolving characters, dramatic climaxes, and shattering suspense scenes. His ballet, *Parade* (1917), with its circus atmosphere, its acrobat, its little girl riding a bicycle, its alliance of painting, dance, and music, was revolutionary, as was his equally outrageous plotless and anticlimactic *Wedding on the Eiffel Tower* (1921). Nor are there any flesh and blood characters or organic, coherent building of episode upon episode, or empathetic involvement, in the works of

136

Tristan Tzara, another of Stein's friends. The founder of Dadaism (1916), Tzara assaulted Western linguistic tradition by rekindling the ancient magic that words originally possessed, restoring to them their ritualistic and incantatory power. In his nonlinear play, *The Gas Heart* (1920), through his cast of characters each a part of the face—Ear, Mouth, Eye, Neck—he demolished theatrical structure and hierarchy, believing that everything was of equal significance. Just as innovative was *If You Please* (1920), a highly charged play by André Breton, the founder of surrealism (1924), and Philippe Soupault, which conveyed the absurdity and eroticism of life, using cutting, jarring, and discontinuous dialogue—techniques to unleash formerly repressed unconscious impulses.

Antonin Artaud, the creator of the "Theatre of Cruelty," derided everything that was logical. He warned his listeners and readers: "Beware of your logic, Sirs, beware of your logic, you don't know to what lengths our hatred for the logical can lead us." His *Jet of Blood* (1925), a play based on myth, symbols, and signs, aimed at rejecting verisimilitude, thus activating a person's "magnetic" nervous system to enable him to project feelings and sensations beyond the usual limits imposed by time and space. As for Artaud's friend, Roger Vitrac, his *Victor* (1928), with its fragmentary visions and divided sequences, left audiences questioning, dissatisfied, frustrated. There were others: Armand Salacrou (*A Circus Story,* 1922), Louis Aragon (*The Mirror-Wardrobe One Fine Evening,* 1923), René Daumal (*En Gggarrrde!* 1924), Roger Gilbert-Lecomte (*The Odyssey of Ulysses the Palmiped,* 1924), Jean Anouilh and Jean Aurenche (*Humulus the Mute,* 1929), and many more.

Although anti-representationalism and anti-traditionalism was in the air, Stein's plays and operas were in many ways uniquely her own. Like her contemporaries, she advocated anti-naturalism in the performing arts: no plot; directionless happenings; no characters; non-referential, and therefore self-contained movement; no logic in the sequence of events; no transitions; no connections; no sense of progress. Rather than espousing mimetism, she sought through the devaluated word to create a fantasy world of her own—a magical realm, an atmosphere, a landscape. She was not, as were some Surrealists, fixated on the unconscious. Her reality was composed of abstract temporal and spatial positions lived in a *continuous present* (the now) and preoccupied

with questions of *identity*. Actors, for Stein, were words. Action
was inherent in the movement created by the hearing or reading
of one word (or sequence of words) in connection to another. "I
tried to tell what happened without telling stories so that the essence of what happened would be like the essence of the portraits,
what made what happened be what it was."[1]

Because most of Stein's seventy-seven plays lack theatrical conventions, such as dialogue, patterns of action, protagonists, climaxes, she felt "that if you write a play you ought to announce
that it is a play and that is what I did." How else would audiences know that her non-characters, whose habits or speech remained unidentifiable, were elements of drama? Could her
disembodied system of voices, often jabbering about nothing in
staccatolike and emotionless meditations, in narrativeless and
plotless illogical sequences, be labeled plays? Was what she
sought to accomplish in the field of dramatic arts—"without telling what happened . . . to make a play the esence of what happened"—really theater?[2] The question is moot.

Stein's first play, *What Happened, a Play* (1913) may, perhaps
answer some of these questions affirmatively. This five-act dialogue drama, written after Stein had returned from "a pleasant
dinner party," set out to capture its tenor and mood. The theme
of this dramatic happening (she "realized then as anybody can
know that something is always happening . . . a quantity of stories of people's lives that are always happening") revolves around
that day's banal occurrences.[3] What remained in *What Happened, a Play,* after the disappearance of conventional patterns of
action, was its carefree and natural atmosphere. Such a technique
allowed the spoken language to prevail: the sounds and rhythms
made by the sequence of phonemes, which were intoned either
singly, in clauses, or in sentences. Its collective and detached atmosphere divested of any possible audience or readeridentifica-
tion with the nonexistent characters and nonexistent plot,
introduced a new brand of theatrical event, contemporary traces
of which are evident in actionless and intellectually constructed
salon comedies of Nathalie Sarraute, for example.

Stein's cerebrally fashioned dialogue, mimicking real conversations, although nonempathetic, encourages imagination to roam
freely and a sense of *play* to prevail. *Play* here, must be understood in its generic sense. In Medieval French theater, the word

jeu, meant, game, sport, frolic, jest, and the ability to manipulate people, events, and mood. Stein's dramatic works are just such *jeux* or *plays.* Ribald in their innuendoes, humorous in their impact, cerebral in their puns and word plays, illogical in their shocking non sequiturs, neologisms, alliterations, metaphors, repetitions, and other figures of speech, they are designed to subvert Western theatrical concepts. Unlike in the traditional theater, names of characters are usually either not mentioned or, if they are, they are not set at the left of the dialogue that is, in fact, non-dialogue. Nor do stage directions exist for the most part. The division of Stein's plays into acts or scenes are usually arbitrary—another weapon in her arsenal geared to deride conventional theater.

Although *What Happened, a Play* can boast of possessing human voices, what is of significance for Stein are the tonalities and atmosphere these generate and their ability to flesh out a nonlinear time emerging from the non-dialogue as it is spoken on the stage space. Reminiscent of some of Stein's other works, the nonstory hermeticism evident in *What Happened, a Play,* along with its semantic and syntactical dislocations, and its illogical verbal, imagistic, rhythmic relationships effected in a *continuous present,* make it particularly intriguing. Felicitous as well is Stein's nonreferential and nonassociational use of numbers in this and other plays. Because their representation throughout the text ushers in no associations, and therefore no recall or definition, the numbers and the words that follow stand alone, thus liberated from what Stein looked upon as encumbrances:

(*One.*)
Loud and no cataract. Not any nuisance is depressing.
(*Five.*)
A single sum four and five together and one, not any sum a clear signal and an exchange.
Silence is in blessing and chasing and coincidences being ripe. A simple melancholy clearly precious and on the surface and surrounded and mixed strangely. A vegetable window and clearly most clearly an exchange in parts and complete.[4]

A Curtain Raiser (1913) is also a dramatic abstraction in which words point to tone, place, and time. Like *What Happened, a Play,* an alliance between numbers and words also exists in *A Curtain Raiser:*

Six.
Twenty.
            Outrageous.
Late,
Weak.
            Forty.
More in any wetness.
Six-three certainly.
   Five.
   Sixteen.[5]

What distinguishes *A Curtain Raiser* from *What Happened, a Play* are the qualitative attributes Stein lends to the digits. In so doing, she ushers in a panoply of sensations that interact in a space/time continuum, eliciting in the mind of the reader or spectator the dimensions of a world of infinite possibilities. Mention must also be made of the manner in which the fragmented, single, or clustered words are spoken—or set on the page—as seen in the above extract. Words, as previously noted, are *actors*, endowed with an inner action or energy factor of their own. Although isolated and solitary, the word's impact on itself and other words, triggers a sense of excitement and wonderment in reader and spectator that seems to flow unhampered. As the voices utter their words, they seem enclosed in their own wholeness; yet they succeed, interestingly enough, in fusing stage-space with time-space. The word and its vocalization, despite bewildering and sometimes frustrating ellipses, generate a singularly haunting climate, a unique intensity and density.

A change in Stein's technique is discernible in *White Wines* (1913). Although without action, dialogue, or division into acts and scenes, an ambiguous reference to characters is discernible in its introductory listing. In no way are these characters to be understood as real in the conventional sense—that is, as beings involved in an event. That an oblique mention of them is made at all, as in the following extract, is surprising, since fictional stage reality is nonexistent:

1. All together.
2. Witnesses.
3. House to house.[6]

Is Stein resorting to deception? Perhaps. But did not Jean Genet demonstrate to perfection in *The Balcony* (1958) that all theatrical reality is a deception? Audiences know that at the theater they are entering into complicity with fictional (false) stage happenings. Yet, they want to (and sometimes do) believe in their actuality, as does Stein in her characters in *White Wines*.

Evolving somewhat, in *For the Country Entirely* (1916), Stein actually names her characters, although none is mentioned more than once. The interlocking threads of this noneventful drama are woven during the course of the play, as each creature of her fantasy discovers his or her—always disconnected—needs and desires via a series of letters.

Tone and rhythm become the virtual protagonists in *Ladies' Voices* (1916), a drama divided arbitrarily into acts and scenes.

Yes we do hear one another and yet what are called voices the best decision in telling of balls.
Masked balls.
Yes masked balls.
Poor Augustine.[7]

The disembodied voices, the banality, and flatness of the language, and the equivocality of statements pronounced in an acausal realm, is paradigmatic of Stein's use of stage "conversation." As a dramatic vehicle, this kind of talk (tone/rhythm/word) sets up vibrations and fuguelike schemes within the text itself, which quiver for auditors and readers.

In *Do Let Us Go Away* (1916), characters exist in name only, these appearing to the left of the lines they speak. What they say is not only illogical according to Western concepts, but has nothing to do with the response of the other protagonists—a true *dialogue de sourds:*

(Nicholas.) I used to be hurried. Now I imagine I will not be.
(Theodore.) It is not necessary to dance or sing. Let us sing that song.
            Let us call them their names Nicholas. Theodore we will.
            We are dishonored. We visit one another and say good-bye.[8]

A Movie (1920) is truly an exception to Stein's no-narrative, no-progression, no-direction, no-subject-or-object plays. This slapstick, acausal film scenario has a story line, a climax, and a suspenseful chase sequence. Its plot revolves around a poor American painter living in Paris, who finds himself a job as a taxi driver, then as a secret service agent assigned to work with a Bretonne housekeeper to recover money stolen from the quartermaster's corps.

The core of *Capital Capitals* (1922), with its simplistic speeches, wordplays, internal rhymes, banalities, lilting and startling rhythms, consists of a long dialogue among four (Arles, Les Baux, Aix, and Avignon) and the trite goings-on in these areas of France.

We have often been interested in the use of the word capital. A state has a capital a country has a capital. An island has a capital. A mainland has a capital. And a portion of France has four capitals and each one of them is necessarily on a river or on a mountain. We were mistaken about one of them.[9]

Virgil Thomson's music for *Capital Capitals*, written in the key of C for two tenors, a baritone, and a bass, with few chords and little harmony, was innovative. The four men's voices, singing frequently in counterpoint or in rounds, injected a sense of excitement into Stein's ritualistic and repetitive style. Thomson noted:

My theory was that if a text is set correctly for the sound of it, the meaning will take care of itself. And the Stein texts, the prosodizing in this way, were manna. With meanings already abstracted, or absent, or so multiplied that choice among them was impossible. There was no temptation toward tonal illustration. . . . You could make a setting for sound and syntax only, then add, if needed, an accompaniment equally functional.[10]

Although Stein's language in *Capital Capitals* was at times purposefully lyrical and sensual, she was, nevertheless, distrustful of tone as a theatrical vehicle. The "beauty of the sounds" the "extraordinary melody of words" emanating from speech are like a trap, a "temptation," luring spectators into a receptive mood and thus obliterating their capacity for objectivity and thought. She wrote:

This melody for a little while after rather got the better of me. . . . I did begin to think that I was rather drunk with what I had done. And I am always one to prefer being sober. I must be sober. It is so much more exciting to be sober, to be exact and concentrated and sober. So then as I say I began again. . . .

Melody should always be a by-product it should never be an end in itself it should not be a thing by which you live if you really and truly are one who is to do anything.[11]

Four Saints in Three Acts (1927), Stein's best-known play/opera, for which Thomson wrote the score, was staged with much brouhaha in 1934, first in Hartford, Connecticut, and then in New York. Its success, some critics explain, was due to its black cast, chosen "purely for beauty of voice, clarity of enunciation, and fine carriage," the popularization of a key line from the work, "pigeons on the grass alas," the cellophane scenery created by Florine Settheimer, the choreography by Frederick Ashton and John Houseman, and its conductor, Alexander Smallens.

Thomson's music was simple, basic, and sophisticated, gliding rapidly from one tonal fraction to another, never solving or settling into a harmonious or accommodating cadence. His was a seemingly perfect orchestration of Stein's verbal voices, her silences, and the strange rhythmic sequences in the successions of excited movement and immobility. Thomson, who strongly believed in the kinship of music and speech, was also aware of its limitations, particularly with regard to Stein's complex tonal and rhythmic effects.

When broaching a Stein work Thomson was, as always, excited at the prospect of discovering new dimensions in sonance and frequency capable of intensifying and magnifying the word's inherent energy. It was he who commissioned Stein to prepare a libretto for him. Having rejected her suggestion of the theme of George Washington and American history, after much debate they settled upon the motif of saints and sainthood. Always drawn to the idea of saints—people who were "better than others"—Stein chose Therese of Avila and Ignatius of Loyola for her protagonists. Uncertainty revolves around the identity of the other two saints mentioned in the title: were they St. Chavez and St. Settlement or two of the many others figuring in Stein's text?

The play consists of a series of meditations enunciated by a narrator-chorus (Stein) and a chorus of saints. Because a person's mental outlook, Stein maintained, is related to and to a great extent formed by one's country of birth, its geography influences his or her qualities and characteristics. Dialogue in *Four Saints in Three Acts,* and other plays of this type, was replaced with what Stein termed, *landscape,* consisting of Avila, for Saint Therese, and Barcelona, for Saint Ignatius. She explained *landscape* as follows:

I felt that if a play was exactly like a landscape then there would be no difficulty about the emotion of the person looking on at the play being behind or ahead of the play because the landscape does not have to make acquaintance. You may have to make acquaintance with it, but it does not with you, it is there and so the play being written the relation between you at any time is so exactly that that it is of no importance unless you look at it.[12]

As the saints speak their minds, Stein makes good use of repetition, rhyme, satire, witticism, childlike listings, verbiage, punning, and ellipses. They become the landscape:

All the saints that I made and I made a number of them because after all a great many pieces of things are in a landscape all these saints together made my landscape. These attendant saints were the landscape and it the play really is a landscape.

A landscape does not move nothing really moves in a landscape but things are there, and I put into the play the things that were there.[13]

Four Saints in Three Acts opens with a somewhat lyrical prologue, outlining Stein's theatrical system: the problems involved in the writing of the play, her doubts as to its worth, and her optimistic final view of the finished work. The mention of her writing technique, revealing a subtle change from narrative and indirect discourse to play writing, not only accounts for the substance of the prologue but becomes an intrinsic part of the entire text of her play.

Stein discloses her desire to pave the way for the thematics of her play: "In narrative to prepare for saints." Suddenly a kind of cubistic change in tone and focus occurs: sequences appear of cutouts and verbal collages revolving around domestic activities. They seem to be appended to her first disclosure: "We had intended if it were a pleasant day to go to the country it was a very beautiful day and we carried out our intention." A landscape is then depicted, after which possible ways of proceeding with regard to stage sets and accessories are enunciated:

Imagine four benches separately.
One in the sun.
Two in the sun.
Three in the sun.
One not in the sun.
Not one not in the sun.
Not one. Four benches used four benches used separately.[14]

"Panic" arises: the author, overwhelmed at the thought of facing the problems involved in the composition of the opera, seeks to bide her time by repeating the title, "Four Saints in Three Acts." In so doing, she hopes ideas will come to her, thus giving her the strength necessary to realize her commitment. She decides, perhaps hastily, to insert a "A croquet scene" into the happenings on stage, whereupon she calls on Saint Therese and some of the other saints to enter her stage reality. Outside of their names, the saint/protagonists (how many there are in the play as a whole is debatable) are divested of genealogy and family. The list reads as follows: Saint Martyr, Saint Settlement, Saint Electra, Saint Wilhelmina, Saint Settle, Saint Pilar, Saint Plan. Their probable nonexistence lends, hilarity, ridicule, and complete disbelief to the notion of saint, sainthood, and organized religion in general.

Act I begins with a terrible storm, a satire on the natural cataclysms that typically usher in the epiphanies or miraculous events mentioned in the Bible and hagiographic literature. Stein had read the meditations of Saint Therese, finding her mysticism practical and her discussion of her body's participation in her spiritual sojourns impressive because of their medical accuracy. The paradoxes associated with Saint Therese's adventurous inner turmoil (her twenty-year struggle with the outer world) were transliterated by Stein in such symbolic clauses as "half in and half out of doors" and "half inside and half outside outside the house"; and her passionate wailings, resulting from her conflicts over philosophical notions dealing with immanence (God pervading the world, bringing turmoil to Saint Therese) and transcendence (beyond the limits of ordinary experience, which brought her serenity), by such simple statements as "if to stay to cry."

Stein's Saint Therese and Saint Ignatius, whisked on to the stage as if it were a circus arena, are not to be viewed as historical characters. Rather, they are like clowns or robots, carrying out their antics during the stage happenings. Their presences, verbal intonations, or silences, are, as in Stein's other dramas, like so many detached and autonomous phrases coming out of a nonexistent or, as some term it, magical sphere.

Why does Saint Therese remain silent at the outset of the play? What is there to say? Why must Saint Therese speak—just because she is onstage? Is her protagonist's (or the author's) inability to articulate her thoughts the reason for "Repeat First Act"?

In due course, Stein again calls for the strange "Enact end of an act" as Act I pursues its course for another few pages. Is she borrowing from musical modes, such as they symphony, concerto, chamber music, etc., where it is customary to repeat bars, passages, and entire movements?

What do these restatements imply with regard to the meaning of the play as a whole? And what is the meaning of Saint Therese's quiescence in particular? She refrains from answering: "If it were possible to kill five thousand Chinamen by pressing a button would it be done." Was the question trivial? What, in fact, is the reader or spectator to make of Stein's ambiguous, elliptical, and nonsensical words? (Some critics believe that they refer to an incident in Stein's personal life.)

It has been suggested that Stein feels more kindly disposed to the warm and passionate Saint Therese than to Saint Ignatius Loyola, the founder of the Jesuit sect. Known for his syllogistic reasoning, rational approach to life and people, methodical procedures of argumentation and discussion, unfeeling and unemotional nature, he is identified by Stein with the patriarchal order. He is, she writes, "well adapted to plans and a distance," "not there. . . . staying where. . . . silent motive not hidden." Although attracted to his powerful intellect and to his unswerving zeal and methods of persuasion, few lines are devoted to him and he is "Left to be."

Stein's nondramatic *Four Saints in Three Acts* tells about saints, but not in terms of their stories. Her ever-changing and frequently contradictory plans for her characters (we see Saint Therese seated at first, then "not seated," finally "not seated at once," and Saint Ignatius "standing standing not seated . . . not standing standing") gives the impression of indecision, discontinuity, but also of the immediacy of a text in progress. Since all occurs in the very process of coming to fruition, the dichotomies between the actual writing of the play and its performance are obliterated. Stein's ability to manipulate time schemes—the past (writing of the event) is transformed into a present (in the performance)—is equally ingenious.

Aside from Stein's technical innovations, *Four Saints in Three Acts* may be understood as a nonreligious ontological piece dealing with the difficulties facing both a playwright and a thinking individual intent upon probing the meanings of the life experience. Like a cubist painting, Stein's vision and verbal gyrations are cut up, fragmented, discontinuous, each moment to be fleshed out, juxtaposed, antithesized for its own unique livingness. Uninterested in Saint Therese's childhood, youth, or adulthood, Stein projects upon characterological factors via images of rain, snow, and water, thus underscoring in her own special way her protagonist's confusion and conflictual nature that seemingly both fascinated and haunted the author. Yet, sharp differences between Saint Therese and the author become obvious in the text: unlike the Saint who withdrew into a convent, hoping to expunge her turmoil, Stein believes in fighting for a cause in the marketplace, while also accepting the vagaries implicit in the empirical world. When it comes to revealed religion, opposition between Saint Therese, Saint Ignatius, and Stein becomes overt: the latter rejects what she believes to be fruitless theological disputations ("How many windows are there in it" "How many windows and doors and floors are there in it"); arid commentaries on the notion of the Trinity ("Having arranged magpies so only one showed and also having arranged magpies so that more than one showed"); and on the Holy Ghost ("magpie," "pigeons"). An enemy of organized religion, Stein's spiritual needs are filled by the experience of transcendence through the immanence operating during the creative process.

Saint Plan. Made it with with in with withdrawn.

Let all act as if they went away.

Viewed as a series of detached moments, *Four Saints in Three Acts* becomes lively, playful clowning clothed in the author's idiosyncratic verbal techniques ("Virgil Virgil Virgil virgin virgin"). Her amusing enumerations ("One two three four five six seven all good children go to heaven some are good and some are bad one two three four five six seven."); her use of homonyms ("Add sum.

Add some."); repetitions; illogical anaphoras ("Four saints are never three. / Three saints are never four"); rhymes ("In time and mine." "Might be third. Might be heard"); assonances ("In clouded. / Included.") are unique in theater. Her listings (some are two pages long), particularly with the intermingling of real and false saints, along with a separate cataloguing of male and female characters—clearly a satire on the manner in which casts are presented on scripts and programs—likewise are also inventive and hilarious. One also wonders whether the one, two, or no lines spoken by a character during the course of the play is to be seen as a pretext for their very existence. But do they exist? Is ambiguity an aspect of Stein's clowning technique? Few if any readers or spectators can identify a protagonist, either by the lines spoken or from his or her presence on stage.

Stein's tapestried verbal structure, which is *Four Saints in Three Acts,* arouses interest because of its timeless quality, its powerful sense of *immediacy.* Although grounded in landscapes, few clues allude to the Spanish countryside. The multiple verbal games, puzzles, images, symbols, numerical sequences, cacophonic/melodic encounters, and masses of words flung throughout the pages, belong to a collective and timeless no-man's land. Even its genre defies definition. Is *Four Saints in Three Acts* a play? game? farce? circus? satire? joke? puzzle set to music? Is the title itself a quip? a caper? There are more than four saints. There are eight and not three acts even though the libretto calls for four: three first acts, two second acts, two third acts, and one fourth act. Is it an arithmetic game? Who has the last laugh?

Dr. Faustus Lights the Lights (1938), Stein's interpretation of the Faust legend, is stylistically and syntactically characteristic of her other works in its repetitions, internal rhyme schemes, flat and ritualistic clauses. It is different in that its verbal hermeticism is to a certain extent understandable and coherent.

At the outset of the opera we see Stein's Faust, the inventor of the electric light, standing "with his arms up at the door lintel looking out, behind him a blaze of electric light."[15] The dim luminosities enclothing him is a visual transliteration of the boredom that has set in following his momentous scientific discovery. Was he right in selling his soul to the devil in return for knowledge? The question as to whether he even has a soul also comes up.

Mephisto, who is onstage, listens to Faust's endless litanies, reassuring him every now and then: "But Doctor Faustus dear yes I am here," to which he retorts: "What do I care there is no here nor there. What am I."

Both Stein and Doctor Faustus are preoccupied and virtually obsessed with questions of identity in a continuous attempt to discover the meaning of life: "there is no hope there is no death there is no life there is no breath, there just is every day all day and when there is no day there is no day."

As previously noted, Stein had explored the notion of identity in *The Geographical History of America; or the Relation of Human Nature to the Human Mind* (1936). Some of her problems in dealing with the question on a personal level were ironed out to a great extent by her division of the personality into two spheres: *Human Nature* (which clings to identity, personality, memory, and a sense of others) and *Human Mind* (which has no identity, every moment "it knows what it knows when it knows it.") The latter, encompassing the Creative Mind, is considered whole, complete, and *absolute existing*, without any need of that other. Because the *Human Mind* is synonymous with the deepest spheres within the human species, it is liberated from time, identity, memory, and other limitations, and, therefore, is capable of bringing forth masterpieces. Stein underscores the differences between *Human Nature* and the *Human Mind* in her now-famous statement:

> I am I because my little dog knows me.
> Which is he.
> No which is he.
> Say it with tears, no which is he.
> I am I why.
> So there.
> I am I where.[16]

As Stein probes the dichotomies between *Human Nature* and *The Human Mind,* she also keeps questioning and intimates repeatedly that to know oneself fully is virtually an impossibility.

Stein's explorations of the question of identity are applicable to *Doctor Faustus Lights the Lights.* Her protagonist wonders whether his invention of the electric light helped him to understand himself better? Whether it brought him fulfillment? What does his invention of *light* symbolize, one may ask? And answer: knowledge, certainly, as well as perception, spirituality, and consciousness. As an inventor, Doctor Faustus is looked upon as a superior being. He is also the prototype of the identityless contemporary person. Aren't Stein's three names for him—Faust, Faustus, and Dr. Faustus—symptomatic of his inability to find out who he really is, resulting in so much of his anguish? We learn during the course of the drama that Faust experiences no peace or inner harmony. He is frustrated. And with all of his knowledge, he still does not know the meaning of the talking dog's utterings of "Thank You." Nor does he understand the reasons behind his appearances and disappearances. And what does the little boy who plays with the dog represent? And who is the single maiden with the dual names—Marguerite Ida and Helena Annabel?

Although Faustus tries to negate the thinking process when he says, "I shall not think / I shall not / No I shall not," he nevertheless seeks to *know* more: namely, that *other* half of life (the feeling or emotional world) he had neglected during his years of intense study. Because emotions are not predictable, they are antirational. As such, Westerners have identified the world of affect with *hell:* with what the conscious mind labels the *shadow,* or that unconscious, fearful, negative, and unfathomable realm that lives inchoate within each individual.

Everything in *Doctor Faustus Lights the Lights* is experienced in Stein's *continuous present.* The dual-identitied Marguerite Ida and Helena Annabel introduces herself as two characters, though she is only one, in a *now:* "I am I am and my name is Marguerite Ida and Helena Annabel." To emphasize the *continuous present,* Stein changes tempo, speech, and thematics ever so gradually, accomplishing the stunt via verbal ambiguities, prolongations, modifications, and repetitions.

Rather than inflate the crisis, when Marguerite Ida and Helena Annabel begins her premonitory song about a viper and is eventually bitten by it, Stein actually deflates it by fleshing out the situation:

Do vipers sting do vipers bite
If they bite with all their might
Do they do they sting
Or do they do they bite
Alright they bite if they bite with all their mite.

Elliptical and oblique allusions to Faust's strange healing methods as he restores the poisoned and dying maiden to health through hypnosis, despite the fact that he cannot see her, reduces the impact of the event to virtual non-interest, nonsense, as well as "fun-sense." So grateful is she to him for his gift of life, that she decides to spend the rest of her days in religious devotion. Temptation, however, soon rears its ugly head in the person of a "man from over the seas." That Mephisto is the one to save her honor is particularly humorous in view of the role he played in the medieval tale: he was instrumental in Faust's seduction of Marguerite, which terminated in her death and final redemption.

Another comic element in the play is the maiden's religious medal, associated with the mystery of her faith, which turns out to be neither cross nor rosary, but rather an artificial viper. That Faust is humbled in Stein's version of the original myth is manifest when the maiden claims to be able to change night into day; thus he is encouraged to confess that he was not the only inventor of the electric light.

The constantly anguished and unfulfilled Faust is further disgraced when he informs Mephisto of his desire to journey to hell. Before he can attempt such a feat, Mephisto tells him, he must commit a sin. He does: he kills the boy and the dog. So energized is he by this act, which he considers paradigmatic of his mastership over his destiny, that he sees himself as having broken free of Mephisto's domination. That he is neither master of his fate nor equal to the task of journeying to hell on his own is evident when once again he yields to the devil's ruseful temptation to become young again and take the maiden with him on his journey. Once youth is restored to Faust, the maiden, surprisingly, rejects his advances. Instead, she falls in a faint right into the arms of the man from over the seas. Further to humiliate the inflated Faust and to demonstrate his incapacity to carve out his own destiny, Mephisto carries him in his arms to hell.

Once in hell, a sphere equated with the unconscious, that is, with the unlimited unknown, Faust in his solitude is compelled to face himself. Alone, he finally understands that he not only is cut off from everyone, but, like a Beckettian character, he lives his life enclosed within his own head. The *light* he had invented, he comes to realize, has not enhanced his understanding of the world nor brought him the serenity for which he longed. Rather, it had the opposite effect. Light, viewed as knowledge, encouraged him to question, to probe still further. No matter what he does, thinks, or feels , the very notion of consciousness must be under-

stood, he finally realizes, *in terms of others* and not only of oneself. He must be conscious of something, of someone:

Leave me alone let me be alone, dog and boy boy and dog leave me alone
let me be alone
    and he sinks into the darkness and it is all dark and the little boy and
    the little girl sing
Please Mr. Viper listen to me he is he and she is she and we
    are we please Mr. Viper listen to me.

Events and relationships in *Doctor Faustus Lights the Lights,* as
in all of Stein's plays and operas, are intertwined and conveyed in
her usual flat, unemotional tones. So, too, are the philosophical
inquiries into the pain and conflict, which *light* (knowledge)
brings in its wake. Although such an opening up of the mind and
psyche activates conscious and unconscious spheres, and foments
a desire to learn and discover, it also increases frustrations as
obstacle upon obstacle comes to light, thereby impeding one's
search.

Might Stein, like Faust, not have concluded that solitude and
loneliness, though painful, as is *light,* have their positive side? Or
was Stein, alluding to the ever-increasing scientific and technolog-
ical advances of the twentieth century, yearning, like Faust, for
darkness and less light?

I sold my soul to make it bright with electric light and now no one not I
not she not they not he are interested in that thing and I and I I cannot
go to hell I have sold my soul to make a light and the light is bring but
not interesting in my sight and I would oh yes I would I would rather go
to hell be I wish all my might and then go to hell oh yes alright.

6

XXXXXXXXXXXXXXXXXXXXXXXXXXXXXXXXXXXXXXXXXXXXXXXXXXXXXXXXXXXXXXXXXX

Fact and/or Fiction

What constitutes a novel for Stein? Does she define it in keeping with nineteenth-century standards? Are her novels based on fact? on fiction? Are they studies of certain psychological types? Do they have flesh-and-blood characters? suspenseful incidents? plots? descriptions? Are the following works, as commonly alluded to, really novels? *The Making of Americans* (1902–11), *A Long Gay Book* (1900–1912), *Many Many Women* (1910), *Matisse Picasso and Gertrude Stein* (1911–12), *A Novel of Thank You* (1925), *Lucy Church Amiably* (1927), *Blood on the Dining-Room Floor* (1933), *Ida, A Novel* (1940), *Mrs. Reynolds* (1940–42), *Brewsie and Willie* (1945).

The Making of Americans may be viewed as a kind of tapestry in which Stein interweaves, in muted and hermetic verbalizations, her psychological, aesthetic, economic, and sexual theories. The action and sub-action revolve around two families (Dehnings and Herslands), their relatives, and their friends.

Of particular interest in *The Making of Americans* is Stein's *anti-novel* technique. Willfully abandoning the conventions of a genre that had reached its pinnacle in the nineteenth century, she does away with plot, characterization, descriptions, and logical sequences of events, substituting for these her increasingly provocative linguistic and stylistic inventions. Although some realistic details are offered the reader at the outset of *The Making of Americans*, thus likening it just a bit to traditional social fiction (such as Émile Zola's *The Rougon-Macquart*, Balzac's *Human Comedy*, or Thomas Mann's *Buddenbrooks*), let the reader beware. These vanish. As a replacement, Stein offers the narrator's continuously present voice, which lends, so Stein believed, a collective or mythological cast to the so-called history of a family.

Unlike the traditional novel, Stein's anti-novel does not build suspense nor is there any causal chain implying progress or deterioration in the happenings. What is emphasized is the uninteresting routine and banal problems of family members and friends. Significant as well is the fact that once the many characters, bobbing up and down here and there, seemingly without rhyme or reason, have spoken their lines, they sink into oblivion: on the collective level, along with the "everyones," the "anyones," and the "some ones." Because Stein applies a kind of leveling process—not one action, person, or object is considered more important than the other—only two characters out of a multitude stand out: Julia Dehning and Alfred Hersland.

Sometime there is a history of each one, of every one who ever has living in them and repeating in them and has their being coming out from them in their repeating that is always in all being. Sometime there is a history of everyone.[1]

Because Stein's intent changed during the course of the writing of *The Making of Americans*, it may be considered a paradigm of her aesthetic evolution. Her digressions, repetitions, rhythms, asides, and puns increase as she attempts to ferret the ins and outs of human personalities. In that they are genetically programmed, the "tempers" of her disembodied characters do not change, though their "mixtures" may vary ever so slightly:

There are many that I know and I know it. They are many that I know and they know it. They are all of them themselves and they repeat it and I hear it. Always I listen to it. . . . They repeat themselves now and I listen to it. Every way that they do it now I hear it.

Voices, tones, and the rhythmic harmonies or cacophonies engendered by the personalities involved had always fascinated Stein.

I began to get enormously interested in hearing how everybody said the same thing over and over again with infinite variations . . . until finally if you listened with great intensity you could hear it rise and fall and tell all that there was inside them, not so much by the actual words they said or the thoughts they had but the movement of their thoughts, endlessly the same and endlessly different.

As in her previous writings, autobiographical elements are also interwoven in subtle disguise. Like Adele in "Q.E.D." and Melanctha, Julia and Alfred are also unable to love due to some kind of rhythmical and tonal incompatability between them. To attempt to root out the origin of such discordance, Stein goes back three generations, to Europe, where she discovers the origins of the character traits that *made* them as they are, that endowed them with their "bottom nature."

There was then always in me as a bottom nature to me an earthy, re-sisting slow understanding, loving repeating being. As I was saying this has nothing to do with ordinary learning, in a way with ordinary living. . . .
As I was saying learning, thinking, living in the beginning of be-ing men and women often has in it very little of real being. Real being, the bottom nature, often does not then in the beginning do very loud repeating.

The transformation occurring from one generation to another, though almost indiscernible, depends upon the way consciousness (which sorts out the quantities of pulsations received) accepts or rejects whatever comes into focus. Changes in attitudes or behav-ioral patterns are made evident by means of Stein's use of conven-tional or distorted grammatical structures (multiple conjunctions and clauses devoid of information) and her patterned use of tenses (past moving into a present frame suggests a change from the chronological time of pure narration to the immediacy of the discursive moment).[2] Verbs become active, energizing forces, sug-gesting greater understanding within a temporal time scheme: "Always more and more I am understanding."

Although Stein's psychological, lexical, and grammatical tech-niques may not have worked in her favor, particularly in her monumental *The Making of Americans*, "[T]o shorten it would be to mutilate its vitals, and it is a very necessary book," as Katherine Anne Porter wrote.[3] And although Stein did admit in time that her systematization of types fell short of her goal, it must be conceded that she had come a long way as an artist!

Stating her purpose in writing *A Long Gay Book*, Stein noted that it was "to describe not only every possible kind of a human being, but every possible kind of pairs of human beings and every possible threes and fours and fives of human beings and every possible kind of crowds of human beings."[4] Understandably, her intent was impossible to fulfill and she did not complete her textbooklike study. Nor did she realize until relatively far into her book that, when dealing with the human personality in novel form, one is not observing a static organism nor can one maintain the objectivity of a scientist peering into a microscope. As in all else, be it in terms of the supergalactic or the subatomic spheres, the mind is incapable of fathoming everything. What Stein did accomplish in this narrativeless and excruciatingly dull work was to list and label psychological types and their characteristics. No landscape, no action, no dialogue, no characters can be said to exist in A Long Gay Book. It has been suggested, however, that when two or more names were mentioned in close proximity to one another, a character relationship might be established.

Strikingly evident in A Long Gay Book is Stein's idiosyncratic language, filled with puns, alliterations, and wordplay. Most innovative and intriguing, however, are her pages and pages of nonmimetic rhythmical repetitions, set down in virtually scientifically planned diagrammatic sentences replete with participles, gerunds, and impersonal pronouns. Although cerebral in the tightness of its structuralization, the impression of playfulness and inventiveness is difficult to surpass. Indeed, the very title, A Long Gay Book, is a play on words: gay suggesting both homosexuality, wantonness, as well as joy, liveliness, and lightheartedness. Less frisky and mischievous is that serious side of Stein's personality, evident not only in A Long Gay Book but also in her novellas, portraits, and plays. In keeping with her scientific training, Stein reiterates her need to pinpoint the difficulties involved in semantics, in the reduction of everything in the text to the present moments, and in the very process of writing fiction—which in reality is not fiction since it studies the typologies of people she knew. Nor is it really a scientific document, since facts have yielded to the power of words.

Like fiction, and implicit in the traditional novel form, some poignant notes are discernible in A Long Gay Book. Writing of her really obsessive desire to discover the elements constituting a human being's "fundamental nature," she reveals a powerful, almost desperate need to understand more about others so as the better to *know herself*.

Every one of the kinds of them has a fundamental nature common to each one of the many millions of that kind of them a fundamental nature that has with it a certain way of thinking, a way of loving, a way of having or not having pride inside them, a way of suffering, a way of eating, a way of drinking, a way of learning, a way of working, a way of beginning, a way of ending.[5]

A certain wistfulness—even regression—can be felt in Stein's evocations of babyhood:

One way perhaps of winning is to make a little one to come through them, little like the baby that once was all them and lost them their everlasting feeling. Some can win from just the feeling, the little one need not come, to give it to them.

Scientific acuity and intense consciousness on Stein's part encouraged her to reaffirm her intent to choose, evaluate, and compare the irritants, anxieties, and uncertainties that mark empirical reality. Although complete annihilation of her past would have facilitated her task, there were moments, during moods of weakness and passivity, when she yearned to relive the "helpless" baby state, prior to the birth of consciousness. Even her early adolescence, despite much of its unpleasantness, still was a source of comfort to her. During the formative years, a child sees itself as *whole;* a sense of inner unity rather than fragmentation prevails in the personality. There is no need to deal with problems of life and death, identity, and alienation, since these are nonexistent in a self-contained being. Emotional sloth, however, ran counter to Stein's better judgment and soon she rejected the luxury of basking in despondency in favor of an energetic approach to life and a desire for "a new beginning."

Stein's mood changes, outlook, and emotional needs are evident in the alterations effected during the writing of *A Long Gay Book.* At the outset of the novel, Stein's chartings and so-called objective classifications of character are clear and precise. As the book proceeds, however, these become increasingly subjective and nebulous. Rather than studying single individuals, as had been her stated aim, "pairs of people" from all walks of life are probed in increasing detail and in typically Steinian listings. The meaninglessness and confusion, not to mention the monotony provoked by the plethora of disembodied names, appearing as they do without seeming plan or purpose, increases with each succeeding page. One may also suggest that her prose at times is devoid of substance: "Meaning something is something. Meaning something and telling that thing is something." Yet, content is nevertheless present, as in her conclusion: "Not coming to anything is something."

Other changes in direction and purpose may also be noted in the writing of *A Long Gay Book*. No longer attempting an exploration of diagrammatic, pseudoscientific typologies, she encourages the haphazard to play a larger role in the unfolding of her noneventful novel. Concomitantly, her chanting assonances, alliterations, inner rhymes, wordplays, and nonsensical semantic schemes increase, allowing her imagination she felt, greater freedom: "Once upon a time when there was a word which went there once upon a time there was a pillow." "Four sses are not singular. Four sses are not at all singular." "A baker had a basket and a basket was bigger, there is no baker and a basket is bigger."

A sense of liberation, gusto, and renewed vigor explodes when Stein succeeds in freeing herself from whatever was irksome to her—frequently, her own inhibitions. When, for example, she excreted her negative feelings concerning traditionally rigid syntactical and grammatical laws, against which she had been rebelling against since her Radcliffe days, her verbal gymnastics leaped forth with abandon. Like a high-wire acrobat, she looked out upon the world, then focused on one stunt at a time. One is menstruation, as paradigmatic of a patriarchal society's devaluation of women: "Once upon a time there was a reverence for bleeding." Recall that in ancient tribal societies everything emerging from a human being, be it spittle, blood, semen, or feces, was considered a creative element, both for individuals and for Mother Earth. In later times, staining was considered an unhealthy and flawsome attribute of the female sex. To draw further attention to what Stein considered to be society's unjust affront vis-à-vis women, she resorted to humor and verbal pranks, remarking that *secretion* is something positive that should no longer be kept *secret;* nor should one be ashamed, disgraced, or even "bashful" about such organic functions.

As Stein's sense of liberation increased, she seemed to be drunk—heady—as words catapulted forth, aligning themselves helter-skelter on the page. That her terms, phonemes, and morphemes made no logical sense to the casual reader did not bother

her in the least. Sound and rhythms were her guides, as were the semiotic effects of the letters imprinted on the page. Language was no longer an abstraction involving thought. It had become matter, taken on concretion, and was ready to be molded, shaped, and textured. Association was a factor in Stein's emerging linguistic ecstasy. Like a child reciting nursery rhymes over and over again, so she was hypnotized by continuous repetitions of words and tones. She seemed to gurgle and bubble with rapture at the discovery of the wealth of melodies, diapasons, cadences, and pulsations at her disposal.

No longer interested in writing a history of all types of human beings, *A Long Gay Book* increases in fun and frolic during the very course of the writing process, concluding on both an optimistic and humorous note:

All I say is begin.
A lake particular salad.
Wet cress has points in a plant when new sand is a particular.

By the time Stein completed *Many Many Women* in 1910, she had dispensed with the novel's linguistic frames, boundaries, and limitations. Referential meanings as well as coherency were virtually nonexistent. A verbal speculator, she focused on *words,* thrilled as they cascaded pell-mell onto the paper. What she sought increasingly was *incantation.* Not the significance of words, but rather the intrinsic energy, the unknown dynamism that linked one to another, was of import to her.

She was expecting what she was arranging and was arranging to be saving what she was saving, giving what she would be receiving was feeling what she was receiving in giving what she was receiving. She was believing what she was giving in receiving, and giving what she was receiving and receiving what she was giving she was feeling what she was believing.[6]

Where does such lyrical and perhaps nonsensical verbiage lead? Endowing the noneventful situations with no apparent beginning or meaningful end, Stein has purposefully and drastically done away with any and all sense of evolution, progress, or organic continuity. On the other hand, the associations arising from her verbal gyrations, certainly for Stein and perhaps for readers willing to speculate about them, may trigger some greater reader/ author participation. The combinations of lilting or harsh rhythms, the smooth, velvety, or cacophonous tonalities, work on the nervous system, either hypnotically or gratingly, in the same way as certain childish incantations, nonsense rhymes, or the echolalia and verbiage of schizophrenics. Stein uses phonetics as a means of heightening or slackening tension. The continuous use of nasal tones, such as *ing,* and their prolongation throughout the page or pages, lends a sense of continuity and security to the novel. The open *o*s, and aspirate *h*s serve to inject a certain unearthly quality, an undefined nonmaterial spirituality to the mood of the work:

Any one and any one, one and one and two, and one and one and one, and one and many, and one and some, and one and any one, and any one and any one, any one and any one is one and one is one and one is some one and some one is some one, any one and one and one and one, any one is that one and that one is that one and any one and one, and one and one, any one is the one and the one who is the one is that one.

There are critics, nevertheless, like Edmund Wilson, who, though not necessarily referring to *Many Many Women,* grew annoyed with such *Steinese:* "But already some ruminative self-hypnosis, some progressive slowing up of the mind, has begun to show itself in Miss Stein's work as a sort of fatty degeneration of her imagination and style."[7]

Stein's intentional primitiveness was in essence a highly sophisticated literary technique, reminiscent of the concatenations of Raymond Queneau, another writer searching for new literary forms, genres, and types of rhetoric. (In another medium it is also reminiscent of some of Picasso's work.) Founder of *OLIPO* (Workshop for Potential Literature), Queneau's linguistic investigations took him into the heart of mathematics, into a domain known as *perimathematics.* His publication of computerized perimathematical fiction and poetry resulted in the birth of ultramechanical literary works. Nouns in specific sections of a book in the process of being written were replaced by the seventh noun appearing at random in a dictionary. Puzzling, surely, but incognizant of the imaginative faculties. In this same vein, Georges Perec wrote a novel without using the letter *e.* Certainly a feat, but are the results valid?[8]

Just as computerized poetry takes on a detached and collective quality, so, too, do sections of *Many Many Women*. In the opening lines, for example—"Any one is one having been that one. Any one is such a one"—it is uncertain whether Stein is referring to her identity problem or to that of others, since the sequence is impersonal. By transcending the individual and the subjective, she can broach the problem of loneliness, anxiety, and the pain of alienation and rejection in terms of *all people*, as in the fifteenth-century allegory, *Everyman*. Although her own problems are far from dissipated, their forbidding power is diminished when she realizes that she is not alone in her anguish. Others as well, particularly writers, feared intellectual sterility, trembled at the thought of becoming social pariahs because of their sexual proclivities. To take a stand requires fortitude, and Stein proved her courage. Unlike André Gide, however, who spoke openly about his homosexuality, Stein could only convey her feelings of love for another woman in highly oblique terms. More like Marcel Proust in this regard, she alluded to her lesbianism via association and symbol.

Matisse Picasso and Gertrude Stein (1933), another example of Stein's verbal speculations, revolves around her and her painter friends. Here, as in *Many Many Women*, her experimental narrative again ejaculates in lively verbal gyrations: repetitive syntax, nonlinear, acausal, undetermined, non-referential, fragmented and nonrepresentational sequences. Although giving the impression of being automatically and autonomously self-generated, Stein's phonemes and morphemes form a life of their own.

Yet, with all due respect to Stein's incredible inventiveness, we are hard pressed to discover any aesthetic or even detailed attributes concerning either Matisse or Picasso, save for occasional oblique allusions to color, design, and texture. Punctuated by personal pronoun subjects such as *he* and *they*, she seems to be focusing on the impersonal and solitary world of the writer, painter, or innovator in general:

He did not and all of them did not and any of them would see that a color which was quite attractive could be a color that is very attractive and some of them if they liked it would do it again would see the color again that they had seen and one of them doing very well what he was doing was not killed and he was hurt enough so that he did not walk when he was carried. . . .

Pleasing and not entirely pleasing is when all that is blue is green blue and not a color that is different from green and blue. A pleasant thing is what being selected is not selected when something is old and when something is young, a pleasant thing is not a pleasant thing when something has been selected which is not what that one selecting did not like.[9]

Words such as *disturbing, arranging, larger, dropping, motioning, dividing,* not only punctuate her verbal score, but are used to refer to and depict the various and distinct styles of Matisse and Picasso. How the above words and others are applicable to certain canvases, however, is ambiguous.

Just as Stein changed her linguistic schematization midcourse in *A Long Gay Book,* so a similar alteration of direction was effected in *Matisse Picasso and Gertrude Stein.* Going beyond mere obliteration of referents and indulgence in "if" clauses ("If there is enough to do a certain way comes to be a way that some one receiving something is distributing what he is selling"), she grew increasingly ruthless, disfiguring ever more blatantly traditional syntax. The following are but some of many examples: "See the whale and taste the butter, show the throat and make hands whither, if a nail is long and short then there is an in-between gold fisher." Synesthesia is used to inflate the sensual experience: "Lying in the same position does cause that nice sound." The verbal cubist collage enters into her scheme of things: "As soon as grammar shows a sympathetic fraction then the time to elope is the same as richness." Her verbal imaginings are more than plentiful. Are such lucubrations meaningful? the stuff of fiction? novels? Or are they verbal exercises? Is it metaliterature?

A Novel of Thank You (1925–26) is more hermetic than the previous works discussed. In that Stein approaches words as living entities, as previously mentioned, they take on the allure of protagonists. These all-important *actors* are, then, endowed with character and personality capable of generating excitement and tension. Thus does she rely upon the evocative nature of *words* to trigger their placement in the text and to sound out the melodies and rhythms to which they give rise. "The central theme of the novel," Stein writes, "is that they [words] were glad to see each other." The statement is as cryptic as the verbal experiment that is *A Novel of Thank You.*[10]

Although Stein refers to people she knows (Mrs. Berenson, Mrs. Bertrand Russell, Mrs. Clermont-Tonnerre, Avery Hopwood, etc.) throughout *A Novel of Thank You,* the work in its entirety can be looked upon neither as fact or fiction, nor even as a novel. Rather, it must be envisaged as an experimental work that seeks to conflate genres, to pursue sequences of non-referential and automated phrases, one appended to another without apparent rhyme, reason, or connective value. A devotee of noncoherent language, Stein's animosity toward the traditional novel genre is flagrant. In connection with Victor Hugo, she writes mockingly: "Supposing everybody thinks of Victor Hugo." About the author of *War and Peace,* she notes, "Let me tell how Tolstoy knew about food."

As in *A Long Gay Book, Many Many Women, Matisse Picasso and Gertrude Stein,* but even more pronounced in *A Novel of Thank You,* Stein seems intent to deconstruct the very essence of the novel genre. In pursuit of her goal, she becomes a devotee of "double-talk," which, for some, generates thought, but for others, degenerates into nought. *A Novel of Thank You* should be looked upon as a kind of demonstration of what Stein terms "pure narrative movement"; of investigation of her special theories concerning *landscape;* and an exploration of her antihierarchical system with regard to capital and small letters. Stein awards primary importance to capital letters, while relegating collective significance to small letters, and her choice had psychological as well as social ramifications. As she explains:

We still have capitals, and small letters and probably for some time we will go on having them but actually the tendency is always toward diminishing capitals and quite rightly because the feeling that goes with them is less and less of a feeling and so slowly and inevitably just as with horses capitals will have gone away.[11]

There is much to be said concerning Stein's views relative to the affective nature of sentences and paragraphs. "Sentences are not emotional but paragraphs are. I can say that as often as I like and it always remains as it is, something that is."[12] These words are applicable to her following work, *Lucy Church Amiably* (1927), a surprisingly coherent narrative compared to *A Novel of Thank You.* The ambiguous "Lucy" and "Church" in the title refer to the "little church with a pagoda-like steeple at Lucy in the region of Belley." Although Stein wrote that *Lucy Church Amiably* was "A Novel of Romantic beauty and nature and which Looks Like an Engraving," its childlike language is prolix. Aimless in its structure, charming in its depiction of the landscape near Stein's summer home not far from Bilignin, it can be looked upon as a meditation of sorts. Thornton Wilder wrote that "she [Stein] set aside a certain part of every day for it [meditation]. In Bilignin she would sit in her rocking chair facing the valley she had described so often. . . . Following the practice of a lifetime she would rigorously pursue some subject in thought, taking it up where she had left it on the previous day."[13]

Stein's perception of the world in *Lucy Church Amiably* seems to be twofold: internalization of nature's excitement and beauty, and a concomitant attempt to inject her fervor and viscerality into the word. Because of its *landscape* quality (Stein's identification with natural phenomena), *Lucy Church Amiably* may be alluded to as a religious work in the broad sense of the word: the merging of the individual with the collective, in free and open participation in the cosmos.

Names of towns and cities are mentioned (Chambéry, Grenoble), along with historical figures from the region (the poet Lamartine, the beautiful Mme. Récamier, and the creative gourmet Anthelme Brillat-Savarin); topography (mountains, waterfalls, streams, hills, etc.), and vegetation (thyme, mint, box, fuchsias, sweet peas, mushrooms, etc.) function in their own way, as particles in the very lifeblood and body of Mother Nature. Everything (human and nonhuman) seems to grow, burgeon, then die in the universal round that is existence.

As in her previous fictional/factual works, Stein's characters in *Lucy Church Amiably* also appear in name only. Although divested of being and bone, they exist *in* nature, and thus participate in its cyclicality, as does everything else in life. Although virtually indistinguishable, since characters are not described, they are not single, but rather composite beings, bearing male/female names (John and James Mary, Simon Therese). Thus did Stein reject gender divisionalism, and she may also have been defending her own proclivities and those of asexual saints, disciples, and deities: John, Mary, Simon, Teresa, Christ. That Stein's protagonist, Lucy Church, is both woman and building at first seems strange. It is not, however, since Mother Church is a common reference. Imagistically, the church's "pagoda-like steeple" may be viewed as a phallus, whereas its onionlike shape calls the feminine to mind. Thus does Stein fuse or confuse the mystery in-

volved in the very notion of religion with its continuous reference
to sexual ambivalence and abstinence in such notions as that of
the immaculate conception. But then, as Stein notes, "Lucy
Church may be any one" or anything.

What is of value in Stein's *Lucy Church Amiably* is the continuity and cohesive power of the feelings and preoccupations to
which her meditations gave rise. She dwells on the newness of
language and her need to approach it in a fresh and untarnished
manner:

> Can't you see that when the language was new—as it was with Chaucer
> and Homer—the poet could use the name of a thing and the thing was
> really there? He could say "O moon," "O sea," "O love" and the moon
> and the sea and love were really there. And can't you see that after hun-
> dreds of years had gone by and thousands of poems had been written, he
> could call on those words and find that they were just worn out literary
> words? The excitingness of pure being had withdrawn from them; they
> were just rather stale literary words.

Such is *Lucy Church Amiably*'s centripetal tendency.

Stein had yet another, perhaps surprising, literary penchant and
outlet for her instinct: detective stories, crimes, and puzzles. They
seemed to answer her need for serenity and mental exercise and
her propensity for deductive reasoning. Detective stories were
"soothing because the hero being dead, you begin with the corpse
you did not have to take him on and so your mind was free to
enjoy yourself."[14]

Blood on the Dining-Room Floor (1933) is in no way represen-
tative of the usual detective-story genre. As to be expected, it is of
her own manufacture and, therefore, of keen interest to Steinian
devotees. Written after an event that took place at a hotel in Belley, a town where Stein and Toklas had spent seven summers, the
novel revolves around a possible murder. So shocking did Stein
consider the event that she felt compelled to write about it. The
facts of the case are as follows: Madame Pernollet, the wife of the
hotel keeper, fell out of a window of the hotel and landed in the
courtyard. What seemed so strange, however, was that Mme. Pernollet's body was so speedily whisked away that no one was even
aware of the incident. Was her death murder? suicide? an accident due to the fact that, as some claimed, she was a sleepwalker?
No answer was ever forthcoming since no real investigation ever
took place.

One would think that the detective genre to which Stein had turned would lead to a clear-cut narration of the mystery. Not so. Another meditation of sorts, her prose remains discursive, meandering, and childlike. Although the sentences are shorter, they are imbued with typical Steinian rhythms and speech patterns. The events, which could be considered melodramatic, were alluded to obliquely, via discussions revolving around problems concerning the families of the region, their physical and emotional states, and the well-hidden secrets harbored by these close-lipped country people. Although everyone knew about the tragedy, no one discussed it. Nor does Stein come up with a solution, as is the custom in the traditional detective story. On the contrary, her flagrant distrust of the artificiality and superficiality of literary genres led her to deconstruct the villain, the hero, and the pseudoreasoning of the detective. Her conclusion for *Blood on the Dining-Room Floor*—in rhyme, no less—was "And now, he had been there, when the lady fell, very well." And what of Stein's reaction to the death of Mme. Pernollet, ostensibly her friend? Detached and unfeeling. Nor did her demise really matter since "no one is amiss after servants are changed. Are they."

Humor, banter, frolic, satire, as well as recognizable action are implicit in what might be identified as a heroine in *Ida, a Novel* (1940), inspired, so it is said, by the life of the Baltimore divorcee, Wallis Warfield Simpson, whose power over King Edward VIII was such that he gave up the British throne for love of her. That she was Stein's protagonist is plausible since Mrs. Simpson had lived in Baltimore opposite the flat occupied by Stein and her brother.

Stein, however, and in typical fashion, does not deal with a particular woman, but rather focuses on the problem of identity via a collective figure. Ida calls to mind such fascinating ancient and modern women as Helen of Troy, Dulcinea, Greta Garbo, the Duchess of Windsor—as well as the author herself. That Ida has been divorced several times, obviously alludes to the multiple marriages of the Duchess of Windsor. The plethora of autobiographical details, however, identify Stein with her: her disenchanted, lonely, and orphaned childhood and youth; her Radcliffe days; Paris years; her fear and dislike of men; and her distrust of public opinion in view of the incredible success of the *Autobiography of Alice B. Toklas* followed by the slow, but definite diminution of her popularity. Who was she—Ida? she questioned. Was she her public's creation?

Different from her previous novels, the associative and impressionistic prose in this work is both exciting and poetic in its probing of a personality from multiple vantage points. Building up momentum and cumulative power via sequences of understatements and exaggerations, which cascade forth with torrential vigor or lapse into silence, Stein increases or slackens tension:

> It was a nice family but they did easily lose each other.
> So Ida was born and a very little while after her parents went off on a trip and never came back. That was the first funny thing that happened to Ida.
> The days were long and there was nothing to do. . . .
> She saw the moon and she saw the sun and she saw the grass and she saw the streets.
> The first time she saw anything it frightened her. She saw a little boy and when he waved to her she would not look his way.[15]

We learn that, after the death of Ida's parents, she was sent to live with one and then another relative, yet the reader is never certain of the identity of any of these phantasmagorias. We know only that Ida is always moving and meeting new people, that she is busy doing nothing, yet anxious as to whether she should do what she is told to do or not.

As is common among many children, particularly those who are in need of companionship, Ida created a twin personality—a kind of alter ego. She had always had a mental double: "Ida—Ida." In time, however, her need for warmth and friendship becomes so acute that she allows her fantasy to take root in the real world. "I am tired of being just one and when I am a twin one of us can go out and one of us can stay in." The split in Ida's personality becomes increasingly overt. At eighteen, her double takes on such reality that Ida begins writing letters to her twin. Not only does such an activity bring her solace, but her double soon plays the role of a protective force in her life. When, for example, Ida says or does something to which people might take umbrage, she can always blame her twin.

Humor, that most complex of qualities that always is implicit in Stein's works, it expressed at strange moments. The so-called funny things that happen to Ida are not so amusing. Frightening incidents involving men are plentiful throughout the volume, and although described in pseudocomical cant, reveal that Ida's psyche is deeply disturbed. A man follows her on several occasions; on another, two men who had been hiding behind some trees suddenly jump out; on a third occasion, walking her dog, she stops at the public park and looks through the railing, only to see a policeman bending to look at her. Ida's covert rage against the male in general is made quite evident when a young man gives her a swimming lesson. Standing next to her in the water,

he leaned over and he said kick he was holding her under the chin and he was standing beside her, and he said kick and she did and he walked along beside her holding her chin, and he said kick and she kicked again and he was standing very close to her and she kicked hard and she kicked him. He let go her he called out Jesus Christ my balls and he went under and she went under, they were neither of them drowned but they might have been.

The real/unreal nature of the above-mentioned incidents and others as well suggests a fundamental distrust and dislike of the opposite sex. Yet, the haunting nature of Stein's oft-repeated images, frequently infused with nightmarish, even ghoulish qualities, also reveal an ambivalence vis-à-vis men: an unconscious fear of them as well as an attraction toward their mysteriousness.

The struggle between reality and fantasy increases during Ida's particularly troubling years. When, for example, her twin is awarded first prize in a beauty contest, Ida feels the necessity of formalizing the existence of her alter ego by giving her a name: "Winnie," because she is "winning." Confusion between the two sides of the protagonist's personality (now divided into Ida and Winnie), increases steadily. Unable to control the one or the other, tension reaches such an overwhelming point that she begins hearing voices: "Ida is that you Ida." An army officer, one of many she frequents, remarks: "Winnie is your name and that is what you mean by your not being here," so traumatizing her that she grows faint. Sufficiently recovered, she tells him that her name is not Winnie, but Ida, and that "there was no Winnie." Thus did Ida try to straighten out her life, by integrating her dual personality and thereby avoiding its takeover by Winnie.

Ida married several times. Perfunctorily, as she did everything else, or so it seemed. A career? It will be either nursing or nunning. She rejects them both because "You have to get up early in the morning to be a nun and so although if she had been a nun she could have thought every day about Andrew [one of her husbands] she never became a nun nor did she become a nurse. She just stayed at home."

Ida is not to be looked upon as a mere technical exercise, as were some of Stein's previous works, but as a barometer that measures her own bloodied inner world. Under the guise of flippancy, coldness, and interludes of sadomasochism, we are invited to peer into the real Stein through projection. Never would she lay her heart bare more overtly than in *Ida*, which may be considered one of her finest and most authentic of works—a precursor of Raymond Queneau's exciting, yet puzzling, grotesque, and certainly unforgettable heroine in *Zazie in the Subway* (1959), and of Vladimir Nabokov's witty, intriguing, and ultimately sordid "nymphet" *Lolita* (1958).

Strangely enough, although maintaining what Stein held so dear, her continuous present, *Ida* deals mostly with past events—another indication of Stein's obsession with those early formative days in a child's life. Although stylistically detached and cold, Stein's narrative reveals a condition of extreme emotional distress. Intent upon hiding her new and recurring bouts of anxiety in the face of the growing actuality of World War II, Stein's insecurity was nevertheless increasing. Although maintaining her calm outwardly, the choice of whether to remain in France or return to the United States preoccupied her unconsciously, as had her parents' demise and the breakup of the family earlier in her life.

Mrs. Reynolds (1940–42) is altogether different from *Ida*. Its genre is unclear. Is it a memoir? a meditation? a novel? or an experimental work? Coherence, continuity, and progress in the narrative per se are not characteristic of *Mrs. Reynolds*. As in *Lucy Church Amiably* and other works of the thirties, repetitions and inner rhyme schemes are rampant; motifs revolve around sequences of abstractions; and observations of human and nonhuman phenomena are viewed from multiple angles, thus increasing already-pronounced ambiguities. A fragmented narrative space emerges as the noncharacters in *Mrs. Reynolds* move about endlessly in a continuous present. Chaotic and unsolvable tangential matters shift in and out of pseudoevents. The welter of polymorphous and polytonal *words* rushing here and there in unintriguing and unimportant thematics without beginning, middle or end, as well as the plethora of irrational sequences, serve to obscure the points Stein is seemingly attempting to make.

Stein's pseudotheme in *Mrs. Reynolds* is set down in the very first sentence: "It takes courage to be couragous."[16] Life, be it in the unfolding of routine or in dramatic events, requires fortitude. This was particularly true for Mr. and Mrs. Reynolds who lived through the turmoils of World War II. Unlike the novels of Hemingway or Dos Passos, Stein's nonaction takes place in a nondepicted locale. It is assumed, despite the many characters bearing Anglo-Saxon names, that the country in which the interminable interior and exterior monologues and dialogues are uttered is France. Flashbacks and flashforwards, conveyed in a continuous present, inform the reader that a war is taking place. Danger becomes apparent in mitigated ways—never overtly. Mention is made only of conquest, black market, dearth of food, and feelings of uncertainty and fear.

Stein makes use of Mrs. Reynolds's unconscious fantasies to provoke tragedy as well as comedy. In her protagonist's dreams or her waking reveries, the frequently macabre images conjured up are disturbing to the reader. One day, for example, when Mrs. Reynolds happened "to see three very very large dark red slugs climbing a tree, they moved very very slowly but they did move," Stein, concluding with one of her famous non sequiturs, stops her heroine from looking at clouds. Pseudohumor with an acerbic twist is evident when Mrs. Reynolds, long before her marriage, dreams "that there were five artichokes blooming in the garden," which she feels augurs well for the future Mr. Reynolds. Since no judgmental valuation is offered, the reader does not know whether this prognostication is good or bad.

Angel Harper (Adolf Hitler), a pseudocharacter introduced early in the novel, represents the evil one. The reader is told that Angel used to live in the region, but moved out for some unknown reason. That such a negative person should be named *Angel* (*angelos* in Greek meaning God's messenger), suggests Stein's aversion to such self-proclaimed envoys, whatever their message.

The reader learns, without the benefit of events leading up to the following statement, that, a corporal at the age of twenty-five, "Angel Harper later was a dictator" bent on war and destruction. Although Mrs. Reynolds has never seen Angel Harper, she learns about his murderous childhood character from the villagers. We are told in Stein's discursive text that Angel Harper was a solitary and mentally disturbed child. At nine years of age he asked to have a small prisonlike room (tomb/womb) built for him. An erotic note enters the text when this same aberrant, now fifty-three, "remembered that a long time before when he was twelve he was in a very strange costume, a hat of a girl and an apron of his mother and he was playing with water, he remembered the water was coming out of a faucet and he had on a strange costume and he was playing with water." Further eccentricities are associated with him: his growing hunger for vegetables, potatoes in particular, which he liked to rub raw over his hands, arms, and face. Stein's emphasis on Angel's increasing age is a paradigm of Hitler's ascending power over France. The reader wonders why Angel Harper is neither viewed with anger nor with hatred throughout the volume. Rather, the figure comes across as complex, anxious, distressed, and psychotic.

Mrs. Reynolds, a composite figure, may have been modeled on Stein and Toklas. Like the former, she is "heavy" and "quite plump," likes dogs, American history, landscapes, plants, and natural phenomena. Analogous characteristics with the latter are her homebodiness, emotivity, superstitions, and intermittent hysteria. "Mrs. Reynolds said that she had her ups and downs, and when she had her ups and downs she had her ups she had her downs." Most fortunate for her is her placid, solid, likable, and reasonable husband. A stabilizing force, Mr. Reynolds is always there to calm her, to prevent her tears, and to advise her to go to sleep each time she feels she is getting excited. When Mrs. Reynolds becomes overly tense Mr. Reynolds says: "Oh come to bed . . . when all is said then come to bed, and that said Mr. Reynolds makes a good song."

Stein's unmitigated satire, however, is never more blatant than when the superstitious Mrs. Reynolds, who relies completely on the prognostications of her favorite saints—Saint Odile and Saint Godfrey—and is misinformed by them. She becomes irrational. Aren't such episodes somewhat autobiographical? Toklas and Stein were forever reading the murmurings of one or another saint, particularly during the war years, and planning their activities accordingly. Yet, one may suggest that the ridicule heaped on Mrs. Reynolds each time she yields to her penchant is so obvious, that one tends to conclude that Stein delved into such "holy" sources only to please Toklas.

Mrs. Reynolds liked holiness when it was related to predictions, she pre-
ferred that a man should be a holy man if he was to predict coming
events, no matter how long he had been dead if he had been a holy man
and he predicted coming events.

In like manner, Stein mocks the Gospels: "They said, when you
ring nobody answers and when you do not ring nobody answers."

Superficial and pedestrian, *Brewsie and Willie* (1945), written
after touring the US Army bases at the end of the war, records
conversations Stein overheard and had with American soldiers
and nurses. Its novelty, if one may use such a word, is to be
found, according to some critics, in Stein's ability to capture the
GIs' slang expressions and patterns of speech.

Unfortunately, the many years Stein spent abroad had made her
lose contact with the changes occurring in the American language. Unlike Hemingway, Stephen Crane, William Faulkner, and
others, the very *livingness* of her native language was no longer at
her disposal. Some of the slang she used in her overly long sentences with their seemingly endless independent clauses was dated
and awkward. Gone was that authentic ring that made for
"Melanctha's" uniqueness. What remains in *Brewsie and Willie*
is pedestrian and banal, both stylistically and in its simplistic and
obviously faulty ideological viewpoint.

As in most of Stein's previous works, locales are omitted. Conversations, therefore, take place anywhere (outdoors, indoors,
walking, sitting, in Paris, in Germany, etc.), thus injecting a confusing note to the work. When writing fiction, such ambiguity is
acceptable, but since *Brewsie and Willie* is purported to be fact, a
kind of memoir, such confusion is inadmissible. Still, it must be
conceded that the variety of voices heard are emitted by people in
all walks of life and all areas of the United States, which lends the
text a variety of intonations, rhythms, and diapasons.

Brewsie and Willie, the two main characters, are different ideationally as well as personality-wise. The former, a philosophical
and thinking type who reflects on war in general and its aftermath, sets the themes over which the arguments and discussions
will revolve. Sensitive to certain issues and situations, he can be
moved to virtual tears. In many ways, he represents Stein's thinking. Willie, frequently lacking in restraint, speaks his mind in sar-
castic and hurtful terms. He voices skepticism, anger, and

pessimism, but during the course of the conversations, he changes
his attitude ever so slowly, while still retaining his humor and
ironic bent. Interestingly, he seems to be growing in understanding and, to a certain degree, in compassion. The foot soldiers and
nurses, who speak their ideas, wants, hopes, and fears, broach all
types of topics from the most significant to the most trifling: pea-
nut butter, jobs, sex, money, Negroes, Germans, French, atomic
bomb, etc.

Unfortunately, Stein was no political scientist, nor was she
versed in economics or sociology. When, therefore, she broaches
such subjects, particularly if venting her spleen against the American system, be it in *Brewsie and Willie* or in her memoir, *Wars I
Have Seen,* her arguments are ludicrous, illogical, specious, and
inconsistent. Having chosen, since 1903, to live her life in France,
she knew little about the United States, particularly during the
war years when only slanted information was reported in the
French newspapers. In fact, her views were so naive as to make
one wonder whether she had ever read a history book. She
blames "industrialism" for *all* problems, small and large: "Industrialism which produces more than anybody can buy and makes
employees out of free men makes 'em stop thinking, stop feeling,
makes 'em all feel alike."[17] Isn't it also quite curious to learn that
Stein, while fearing a takeover by industry of what had been
looked upon as American individualism and warned of the imprisoning, destructive nature of the industrial society, was herself
benefiting from the advantages offered by this "nefarious"
power? Indeed, she had always lived from unearned increment:
the clever investments made for her in the United States by her
family. While her rage against capitalism pursued its course, she
was also sending her manuscripts to American publishers, yearning for success in this same land.

Although admiring the courage and fortitude of the American
soldier in *Wars I Have Seen,* Stein, in *Brewsie and Willie,* is vit-
riolic in attacking and condemning the very same beings she had
just seen fit to praise. That she criticized the soldiers' so-called
adolescent ways because they enjoyed sweets, pinups, and liquor,
and labeled them "spoiled babies" who did not know what life
was all about, is understandable since they were young, and surprising, in view of the fact that they had been through excoriating
experiences in a war that Stein had labeled "far more interesting"
than World War I.[18] Irony is compounded: after remarking on

the immaturity of Americans in general, who have lost their thinking capacity and their ability to "articulate," she nevertheless seeks out such nonthinking and money-minded Americans to publish her works! Neither France nor any other European country had embarked on such a financially unremunerative venture as the publication of Gertrude Stein's work. It was the immature Americans who not only read her books but became her most fervent admirers. Had they lost their thinking capacity in this respect, too? Were Americans devoid of taste and aesthetic principles?

To expect logical ideations or sustained and forward-moving discussions from Stein is not possible. Let us in fact recall two statements she made just prior to the outbreak of World War II and shortly after its conclusion. Hitler "was not dangerous because he was only a German romanticist, who wanted the feelings of triumph but would never go through the blood bath to get it." Hitler "was essentially a nineteenth-century person, and his war had destroyed the nineteenth century."[19]

Whether or not, at the conclusion of World War II, Stein was already ill from the cancer that was to take her life, it in no way relieves her of the burden of her blindness in assessing the events leading up to the war. Never did she argue a case or develop an idea or even give reasons for her value adjudications. As an artist she was not called upon to politicize or philosophize, so she should have refrained from broaching significant problems in a cavalier manner. Were Ida to have indulged in puerile comments and multiple quips, readers would have reacted with laughter. That Stein was speaking through Brewsie and Willie elicits pity, but not compassion.

Conclusion

"To have become a Founding Father of her century," wrote Virgil Thomson, "is her own reward for having long ago, and completely, dominated her language."[1] Stein was just that and had accomplished just that. Her incredible achievement was slow in coming, but once realized, it was evident that it was deeply rooted in the literary soil of her time.

Stein had remarked, with a smile of satisfaction, once recognition became hers: "My little sentences have gotten under their skins." And they had. Arresting, intriguing, frustrating, they were also fascinating. Symptomatic of things to come. Why had Stein been so obsessed with language? speech? the word? the sentence and the paragraph? Was it in part because she failed to conform to the rules and regulations of her professors of English at Radcliffe? Some had commented on her faulty spelling, syntax, logic, and continuity of thought processes. She could not, they noted, convey her ideas in a straightforward manner, particularly when emotionally involved in her subject matter. Nor, as I have explained, did her publishers think more highly of her writings.

Perhaps Stein's inability to conform linguistically to the norms of her day was paradigmatic of other levels of rebellion brewing within her. Her fight against conventions to which she could not adapt, however, brought her the pain and misery of solitude and alienation. Through her view of language, she had first hoped to discover the "bottom nature" of people, the better to relate to them. "I had been enormously interested all my life in finding out what made each one that one and so I had written a great many portraits."[2] But then she realized her goal was an impossible one. Because the soundings and resoundings of human nature are infinite, she, as a mere mortal, could not possibly understand them *plain*.

Stein discovered another course. "I like the feeling the everlasting feeling of sentences as they diagram themselves. In that way one is completely possessing something and incidentally one's self."[3] Out of necessity she created her own verbal systems, her own syntax, grammar, and language—and her own way of living her life. The *struggle* in directing such a route was immense: arduous in terms of the loneliness involved in breaking new ground; painful in the many rejections she received from publishers. Only when she realized that her searing hurt was not hers alone, but the lot of every great—and even the not-so-great—creative spirit, did she understand that self-worth is not dependent upon the reactions of others. Once traditional referents had been abolished and syntax disrupted, words, like so many isolated entities, were transformed, becoming detached and heteroclite *signs* and *sounds*. Instead of creating a tapestry with an outwardly or easily understandable logical pattern, Stein proceeded cognitively and sensately to spin her own web as she—and not the masses of readers—understood it.

Only Stein's momentous and sudden leap to fame with *The Autobiography of Alice B. Toklas* and the slow decline that followed finally forced her to accept the fact that readers were and are but a "checkerboard" of separate audiences, as Henry James had said, and that she could not count on them to affirm her own worth or define her own *identity*. "I am I because my little dog knows me."

Stein will also be remembered as a landmark figure: an American ex-patriate in Paris who knew how to attract the best in the arts to her orbit. Her apartment at 27, rue de Fleurus that she shared with her brother, was the center of what was to become in time a star-studded coterie of friends—Picasso, Matisse, Picabia, Gris, Hartley, Thomson, Anderson, Hemingway, Fitzgerald, and others. It was an unforgettable era, that she helped to mold and to mark in her own way.

As art collectors, the Steins were known the world over. Their "junking" expeditions provided them with prints, etchings, drawings, and paintings by Renoir, Delacroix, Toulouse-Lautrec, Gauguin, and Cézanne, the latter, among her favorites. It was in 1905 that she and her brother purchased what has been alluded to as some of the most spectacular canvases of the century, among them, Matisse's *Woman with the Hat;* Picasso's *Young Girl with a Basket of Flowers,* and Cézanne's *Portrait of Mme. Cézanne.*

The impact of Cézanne's canvases on Stein accounted in part for the interdisciplinary turn her writing was to take. His rejection of hieratic and hierarchical values, moods, structures, and meanings were crucial, for example, to the creation of her ground-breaking novella, "Melanctha," and its non-centered and non-framed reality.

Stein's unforgettable verbal portraits of such notables as Picasso, Matisse, Cézanne, Apollinaire, to mention but a few, captured the fundaments of these personalities and their art in elliptical, sometimes highly frustrating, verbal images in which sensation is geometricized and compositional hierarchies are banished, along with the notion of a central idea.

Picasso and his cubist paintings taught her how to emphasize still lifes and use mundane objects as the substance for some of her poems, namely those included in *Tender Buttons*. Like the collages of Picasso, Braque, and Gris, Stein aroused a new reality, a new excitement in the non-relational, non-illusionist word that became for her a *thing* in and of itself.

Stein was also a virtuoso of the theater and opera. Not only did she mock all stage conventions, plot, characterizations, time schemes, syntax, and grammar, but she established new speech, visual, and dramatic connections while also remaking language. Her first play, *What Happened, a Play,* created a collective and detached atmosphere divested of any possible audience—or reader—identification with the nonexistent characters and nonexistent plot. Her opera, *Four Saints in Three Acts,* for which Thomson wrote the score, consisted of a series of meditations enunciated by a narrator-chorus and a chorus of saints who were not really saints. Enigmatic? Certainly. Fascinating? To be sure. Her drama, *Doctor Faustus Lights the Lights,* explored the problems of identity in an equally innovative or outlandish manner. Humor, satire, and continuous punning are implicit in all of her plays—in all of her writings.

That Stein played a significant role in shaping twentieth-century literature is a truism today. Her contribution as we know was antipodal to the well-made novel, play, or poem written for popular consumption and read on a bus, subway, or plane, then discarded in some bin, but rather in the creation of the ever-new, ever-renewing, and ever-renewable *work of art*.

Writing, for her, served as a kind of hiding place where she could secrete her innermost thoughts and feelings. Her prose and

poetry were hermetic and coded. Words, images, rhythms, sonorities served to mask an inner tumultuous world as well as revolutionary literary concepts. By dislocating, deforming, denuding,
and fragmenting what previously had been whole, Stein altered
traditional meanings and emotional reactions to words and epi-
thets, thereby remolding and reshuffling the focus and conventional values of readers. As Sherwood Anderson wrote: "She is
laying word against word, relating sound to sound, feeling for the
taste, the smell, the rhythm of the individual word. She is attempting to do something for the writers of our English speech
that may be better understood after a time, *and she is not in a
hurry.*"[4]

Stein's frequent punning, riddles, double entendres, and general
non-sense may be considered a mockery of language and may
make some of her writings inaccessible. On the other hand, en-
coded works may be intellectually stimulating, opening up readers to a new level of awareness as to the meaning and purpose of
language.

Stein dared to use, manipulate—violate—traditional verbal
configurations and alignments. She ruptured rhythms and images
and flattened contours, thus converting and molding the very in-
gredients that make up clauses, sentences,and paragraphs, to suit
her vision. By nullifying the habitual, she indulged her bent for
meandering, wandering conversational tones. These resulting disembodied movements, existing in a space-time continuum, became the very substance of the *Steinese* event. As William Carlos
Williams noted:

Having taken the words to her choice, to emphasize further what she has
in mind she has completely unlinked them . . . from their former relationships to the sentence. This was absolutely essential and unescapable.
Each under the new arrangement has a quality of its own, but not con-
joined to carry the burden science, philosophy, and every higgledy-
piggledy figment of law and order have been laying upon them in the
past. They are like a crowd at Coney Island, let us say, seen from an
airplane. . . . She has placed writing on a plane where it may deal unhampered with its own affairs, unburdened with scientific and philosophic lumber.[5]

Notes

Introduction

1. Carl Van Vechten, "A Stein Song," *Selected Writings of Gertrude Stein* (New York: Vintage Books, 1972), xxiv.

Chapter 1: The Exile

1. Alfred H. Barr, Jr., *Matisse: His Art and His Public* (New York: Museum of Modern Art, 1951), 53.
2. Herbert Read, *A Concise History of Modern Painting* (New York: Praeger, 1954), 13.
3. Ibid., 17. From *Letters,* edited by John Rewald (London: Cassirer, 1931), 234.
4. Gertrude Stein, *Everybody's Autobiography* (New York: Random House, 1937), 133.
5. Ibid., 9.
6. Alice B. Toklas, *Staying on Alone* (New York: Liveright, 1973), 355. Letter to Carl Van Vechten, December 26, 1927.
7. Gertrude Stein, *Wars I Have Seen* (New York: Random House, 1945), 27.
8. Gertrude Stein, *The Making of Americans* (Paris: Contact Editions, 1925), 426, 424, 488–89.
9. Gertrude Stein, *The Autobiography of Alice B. Toklas* (New York: Vintage Books, 1972), 97–98.
10. Solomon and Stein, "Normal Motor Automatism," *The Psychological Review,* No. 3, September 1896. "Cultivated Motor Automatism," No. 5, May 1898.
11. Richard Bridgman, *Gertrude Stein in Pieces* (New York: Oxford University Press, 1970), 24.
12. Ibid., 22–25.
13. James R. Mellow, *Charmed Circle* (New York: Praeger, 1974), 47.
14. Ibid., 65.

179

15. Stein, *Autobiography*, 66.
16. Irene Gordon, "A World beyond the World: The Discovery of Leo Stein," in *Four Americans in Paris* (New York: Museum of Modern Art, 1970), 26.
17. Ibid., Undated letter to Mabel F. Weeks, 1905.
18. Ibid., From Leo Stein, *Appreciation: Painting, Poetry, and Prose*, 173.
19. Ibid., 52. William Sutton taped interview on basis of Robert Bartlett Hass's *A Primer for the Gradual Understanding of Gertrude Stein*.
20. Stein, *The Making of Americans*, 53–54.
21. Bridgman, *Stein in Pieces*, 47.
22. Leo Stein, *Appreciation: Painting, Poetry, and Prose*, 188.
23. Mellow, *Charmed Circle*, 90.
24. Ibid., 89.
25. Irene Gordon in *Four Americans*. Letter to Mabel Weeks, November 29, 1905, 27.
26. Gertrude Stein, *Gertrude Stein on Picasso* (New York: Liveright, 1970), 30.
27. Leon Katz, "Matisse, Picasso, and Gertrude Stein," in *Four Americans*, 50.
28. Pierre Daix, *Picasso* (New York: Praeger, 1965), 58–59.
29. Mellow, *Charmed Circle*, 93.
30. Stein, *Gertrude Stein on Picasso*, 3.
31. Leon Katz in *Four Americans*, 60, 54.
32. Stein, *Gertrude Stein on Picasso*, 110.
33. Ibid., 96.
34. Leon Katz in *Four Americans*, 60.
35. Stein, *Gertrude Stein On Picasso*, 24.
36. Ibid., 14.
37. Ibid., 114.
38. Gertrude Stein, *Selected Writings of Gertrude Stein*, edited by Carl Van Vechten, 335.
39. Katz, *Four Americans*, 62.
40. Ibid.
41. Stein, *Gertrude Stein On Picasso*, 19.
42. Ibid., 61.
43. Ambroise Vollard, *Recollections of a Picture Dealer* (Boston: Little, Brown, 1936), 137.
44. Ibid., 138.
45. Gertrude Stein, *Everybody's Autobiography* (New York: Random House, 1937), 4.
46. Gertrude Stein, *Matisse Picasso and Gertrude Stein with Two Shorter Stories* (Paris: Plain Editions, 1933), 37. Gertrude Stein, *Geography and Plays* (Boston: Four Seas, 1922), 187.

47. Mellow, 97.

48. Alice Toklas, *What Is Remembered* (New York: Holt, Rinehart & Winston, 1963), 23–24.

49. Ibid.

50. Mellow, *Charmed Circle*, 113.

51. Ibid.

52. Toklas, *Staying on Alone* (New York: Liveright, 1973), 64.

53. Dodge Luhan, *European Experiences* (New York: Harcourt, Brace, 1935), 328.

54. Stein, *Everybody's Autobiography*, 126–27.

55. Ibid., 76–77.

56. Dodge Luhan, *European Experiences*, 327.

57. Gertrude Stein, *Two: Gertrude Stein and Her Brother* 2–34.

58. Ibid., 19.

59. Mellow, *Charmed Circle*, 207.

60. Ibid., 333.

61. Stein, *Gertrude Stein On Picasso*, 96.

62. Gertrude Stein, *Bee Time Vine* (New Haven: Yale University Press, 1953), 78, 92, 110, 112, 87, 91, 100.

63. Ray Lewis White, ed., *Sherwood Anderson/Gertrude Stein: Correspondence and Personal Essays* (Chapel Hill, North Carolina: University of North Carolina Press, 1973), 9.

64. Ibid., 9, 68.

65. Ibid., 10, 17.

66. Ibid., 84, 42.

67. Jeffrey Meyers, *Hemingway, A Biography* (New York: Harper and Row, 1985), 76.

68. Carlos Baker, *Ernest Hemingway: Selected Letters 1917–1961* (New York: Charles Scribner's Sons, 1981), 650.

69. Meyers, *Hemingway*, 78.

70. Ernest Hemingway, *A Moveable Feast* (New York: Bantam, 1969), 15.

71. Baker, *Ernest Hemingway*, 795.

72. Hemingway, *A Moveable Feast*. 20.

73. Meyers, *Hemingway*, 81.

74. Baker, *Ernest Hemingway*, 649.

75. Meyers, *Hemingway*, 78.

76. Baker, *Ernest Hemingway*, 650, 736.

77. Virgil Thomson, *Virgil Thomson* (New York: Alfred A. Knopf, 1966), 91–92.

78. Bridgman, *Stein in Pieces*, 188.

79. *Testimony against Gertrude Stein*, in *transition* (The Hague: Servire Press), February, 1935, 23.

80. Mellow, *Charmed Circle*, 373.

81. Ibid., 424. From *New York Times*, December 5, 1937.
82. Ibid., 372.
83. Toklas, *Staying On Alone*, 42.
84. Stein, *Selected Writings of Gertrude Stein*, 622.
85. Ibid., 616.
86. Ibid., 623.
87. Ibid., 632.
88. Eric Sevareid, *Not So Wild a Dream* (New York: Atheneum, 1976), 455–462.
89. *Life*, "Off We All Went to See Germany," August 6, 1945.
90. Mellow, *Charmed Circle*, 466.
91. Toklas, *What Is Remembered*, 173. *Letters of Gertrude Stein and Carl Van Vechten* (New York: Columbia University Press, 1986), Vol. 2, April 24, 1953, 276.
92. Stein, *The Making of Americans*, 498.

Chapter 2: The Matriarchate and the Lesbian

1. Samuel Steward, *Dear Sammy* (Boston: Houghton Mifflin Co., 1977), 55.
2. Ibid., 56.
3. *New Larousse Encyclopedia of Mythology* (New York: Prometheus Press, 1973), 122. Barbara G. Walker, *The Woman's Encyclopedia of Myths and Secrets* (New York: Harper & Row, 1983), 535.
4. Leo Katz, introduction to *"Fernhurst," "Q.E.D.," and Other Early Writings* by Gertrude Stein (New York: Liveright, 1971), iv.
5. Ibid., vii.
6. Michael J. Hoffman, *Gertrude Stein* (Boston: Twayne Publishers, 1976), 86.
7. Katz introduction, *Early Writings*, xxi.
8. Ibid., xxix.
9. Bridgman, *Stein in Pieces*, 47.
10. Stein, *Selected Writings of Gertrude Stein*, 338.
11. Ibid.
12. Stein, *Two: Gertrude Stein and Her Brother* (New York: Harper Colophon Books, 1970), 15, 135, 100, 45, 57.
13. Stein, *Bee Time Vine*, 77, 78, 79, 80, 83, 91, 108, 87, 96.
14. Ibid., 40.
15. Ibid., 12.
16. Stein, *Selected Writings of Gertrude Stein*, 543.
17. Ibid., 566.
18. Jayne L. Walker, *The Making of a Modernist: Gertrude Stein* (Amherst: University of Massachusetts Press, 1984), 81.

Chapter 3: Verbal Portraits

1. Gertrude Stein, "Portraits and Repetition," *Lectures in America* (Boston: Beacon Press, 1985), 183.
2. Wendy Steiner, *Exact Resemblance to Exact Resemblance: The Literary Portraiture of Gertrude Stein* (New Haven: Yale University Press, 1978), 54.
3. Stein, "Portraits and Repetition," 176.
4. Steiner, *Exact Resemblance*, 42.
5. Alfred H. Barr, *Matisse: His Art and His Public* (New York: Museum of Modern Art, 1951), 119–23.
6. Leo Stein, *Journey into the Self: Being the Letters, Papers, and Journals of Leo Stein* (New York: Crown Publishers, 1950), 58. Letter to Mabel Weeks, February 7, 1913.
7. Gertrude Stein, *Notebooks*, fragment #130. Quoted from Dore Ashton, *Picasso on Art: Selection of Views* (New York: Viking, 1972), 164.
8. Steiner, *Exact Resemblance*, 76.
9. Walker, *Making of a Modernist*, 98.
10. Leo Stein, *Journey*, 53.
11. Vollard, *Recollections of a Picture Dealer*, 138.
12. Stein, "Pictures," *Lectures in America*, 76.
13. Stein, "Plays," *Lectures in America*, 105.
14. Herschell B. Chipp, "Letter to Emile Bernard," 25 October 1905. From *Theories on Modern Art* (Berkeley: University of California Press, 1973), 22.

Chapter 4: *Tender Buttons . . .*

1. Randa K. Dubnick, *The Structure of Obscurity: Gertrude Stein, Language, and Cubism* (Urbana: University of Illinois Press, 1984), 35.
2. Stein, "Poetry and Grammar," *Lectures in America*, 209.
3. Ibid., 235.
4. Walker, *Making of a Modernist*, 132.
5. Stein, "Poetry and Grammar," 231.
6. Katz, "Matisse, Picasso, and Gertrude Stein," *Four Americans in Paris*, 52.

Chapter 5: Theater and Opera

1. Stein, "Plays," *Lectures in America*, 122.
2. Ibid., 118.
3. Ibid.
4. Stein, *Selected Writings of Gertrude Stein*, 557.

5. Stein, *Geography and Plays*, 202.
6. Ibid., 210.
7. Stein, *Selected Writings*, 556.
8. Stein, *Geography and Plays*, 215.
9. Gertrude Stein, *Operas and Plays* (Barrytown, New York: Station Hill Press, 1987), 61.
10. Virgil Thomson, *The Musical Score* (New York: Alfred A. Knopf, 1945), 297–98. See Jane Bowers, "The Writer in the Theatre: Gertrude Stein's *Four Saints in Three Acts*," in Michael Hoffman, *Critical Essays on Gertrude Stein* (Boston: G. K. Hall, 1986), 213.
11. Stein, "Portraits and Repetition," *Lectures in America*, 196–98.
12. Stein, "Plays," 122.
13. Ibid., 129.
14. Stein, *Selected Writings of Gertrude Stein*, 582.
15. Gertrude Stein, *Last Operas and Plays* (New York: Rinehart, 1949), 0.
16. Gertrude Stein, *The Geographical History of America; or, The Relation of Human Nature to the Human Mind* (New York: Random House, 1936), 71.

Chapter 6: Fact and/or Fiction

1. Stein, *The Making of Americans*, 227.
2. Walker, *Making of a Modernist*, 51.
3. Katherine Anne Porter, "Everybody Is a Real One," in Michael J. Hoffman, *Critical Essays on Gertrude Stein*, 50.
4. Gertrude Stein, "The Gradual Making of *The Making of Americans*," *Lectures in America*, 148.
5. Stein, *Matisse Picasso and Gertrude Stein*, 16.
6. Gertrude Stein, *Many Many Women*, appears in *Matisse Picasso*, 175.
7. Edmund Wilson, *Axel's Castle* (New York: Farrar, Straus & Young, 1952), 239.
8. Bettina L. Knapp, *French Novelists Speak Out* (Troy, New York: Whitston Press, 1976), 44–47.
9. Stein, *Matisse Picasso and Gertrude Stein*, 201.
10. Gertrude Stein, *A Novel of Thank You* (New Haven: Yale University Press, 1958), 188.
11. Stein, "Poetry and Grammar," *Lectures in America*, 223.
12. Ibid., 223.
13. Thornton Wilder's introduction in Gertrude Stein, *Four in America* (New Haven: Yale University Press, 1947), ix.
14. Gertrude Stein, *How Writing is Written* (Los Angeles: Black Sparrow Press, 1974), 138.

15. Gertrude Stein, *Ida* (New York: Random House, 1941), 8.
16. Gertrude Stein, *Mrs. Reynolds and Five Earlier Novelettes* (New Haven, Yale University Press, 1952), 1.
17. Gertrude Stein, *Brewsie and Willie* (New York: Random House, 1946), 55.
18. Eric Sevareid, *Not So Wild a Dream* (New York: Atheneum, 1976), 461.
19. Ibid., 460.

Conclusion

1. Carl Van Vechten, "A Stein Song," in *Selected Writings of Gertrude Stein*, xx.
2. Gertrude Stein, "Plays," *Lectures in America*, 119.
3. Ibid., "Poetry and Grammar," 211.
4. Van Vechten, "A Stein Song," xx.
5. Ibid., xxi.

Bibliography

Principal Works of Gertrude Stein

Alphabets and Birthdays. Introduction by Donald Gallup. New Haven: Yale University Press, 1957.

As Fine as Melanctha. Foreword by Natalie Clifford Barney. New Haven: Yale University Press, 1954.

Bee Time Vine and Other Pieces. Preface and notes by Virgil Thomson. New Haven: Yale University Press, 1953.

Blood on the Dining-Room Floor. Foreword by Donald Gallup. Pawlet, VT: Banyon Press, 1948.

Brewsie and Willie. New York: Random House, 1946.

Composition as Explanation. London: Hogarth Press, 1926.

"Cultivated Motor Automatism," *The Psychological Review.* 5 May 1898. With Leon Solomons. 295–306.

Everybody's Autobiography. New York: Random House, 1937.

"Fernhurst," "Q.E.D.," and Other Early Writings by Gertrude Stein. Edited with an introduction by Leon Katz. Appendix by Donald Gallup. New York: Liveright, 1971.

Four in America. Introduction by Thornton Wilder. New Haven: Yale University Press, 1947.

The Geographical History of America; or, The Relation of Human Nature to the Human Mind. Introduction by Thornton Wilder. New York: Random House, 1936.

Geography and Plays. Boston: Four Seas, 1922.

Gertrude Stein: Writings and Lectures 1909–1945. Edited by Patricia Meyerowitz. Baltimore: Penguin, 1971.

Gertrude Stein on Picasso. Edited by Edward Burns. Afterword by Leon Katz and Edward Burns. New York: Liveright, 1970.

How to Write. Paris: Plain Edition, 1931.

How Writing Is Written. Edited by Robert Bartlett Haas. 2 vols. Los Angeles: Black Sparrow Press, 1974.

Ida. New York: Random House, 1941.

Last Operas and Plays. Edited with introduction by Carl Van Vechten. New York: Rinehart, 1949.

Lectures in America. Introduction by Wendy Steiner. Boston: Beacon Press, 1985.

Lucy Church Amiably. New York: Something Else Press, 1969.

The Making of Americans. Paris: Contact Editions, 1925.

Matisse Picasso and Gertrude Stein with Two Shorter Stories. Paris: Plain Editions, 1933.

"Normal Motor Automatism," *The Psychological Review.* 3 September 1896. With Leon Solomons.

Mrs. Reynolds and Five Earlier Novelettes. Foreword by Lloyd Frankenberg. New Haven: Yale University Press, 1952.

A Novel of Thank You. Introduction by Carl Van Vechten. New Haven: Yale University Press, 1958.

Operas and Plays. Foreword by James R. Mellow. Barrytown, New York: Station Hill Press, 1987.

Painted Lace and Other Pieces. Introduction by Daniel-Henry Kahnweiler. New Haven: Yale University Press, 1955.

Portraits and Prayers. New York: Random House, 1934.

A Primer for the Gradual Understanding of Gertrude Stein. Vol. 1. Edited by Robert Bartlett Haas. Los Angeles: Black Sparrow Press, 1971.

Reflections on the Atomic Bomb. Edited by Robert Bartlett Haas. Los Angeles: Black Sparrow Press, 1973.

Selected Writings of Gertrude Stein. Edited by Carl Van Vechten. New York: Random House, 1946. Includes *The Autobiography of Alice B. Toklas, Tender Buttons*, etc.

Sherwood Anderson/Gertrude Stein: Correspondence and Personal Essays. Edited by Ray Lewis White. Chapel Hill, North Carolina: University of North Carolina Press, 1973.

Three Lives. Norfolk, CT: New Directions, 1933.

Two: Gertrude Stein and Her brother and Other Early Portraits. Foreword by Janet Flanner. New Haven: Yale University Press, 1951.

Wars I Have Seen. New York: Random House, 1945.

What Are Masterpieces? Edited by Robert Bartlett Haas. Los Angeles: Black Sparrow Press, 1974.

The World Is Round. New York: William R. Scott, 1939.

Secondary Sources

Ashton, Dore. *Picasso on Art: Selection of Views.* New York: Viking, 1972.

Baker, Carlos. *Ernest Hemingway: Selected Letters 1917–1961.* New York: Charles Scribner's Sons, 1981.

Barr, Alfred H., Jr., *Matisse: His Art and His Public*. New York: Museum of Modern Art, 1951.

——. *Picasso: Fifty Years of His Art*. New York: Museum of Modern Art, 1946.

Blankley, Elyse. "Beyond the 'Talent of Knowing': Gertrude Stein and the New Woman." In Michael Hoffman's *Critical Essays on Gertrude Stein*. Boston: G. K. Hall, 1986.

Bloom, Harold, ed. *Modern Critical Views: Gertrude Stein*. New York: Chelsea House Publishers, 1986.

Bowers, Jane. "The Writer in the Theater: Gertrude Stein's *Four Saints in Three Acts*." In Michael Hoffman's *Critical Essays on Gertrude Stein*. Boston: G. K. Hall, 1986.

Bridgman, Richard. *Gertrude Stein in Pieces*. New York: Oxford University Press, 1970.

Brinnin, John Malcolm. *The Third Rose: Gertrude Stein and Her World*. Boston: Little, Brown, 1959.

Burns, Edward, ed. *Letters of Gertrude Stein and Carl Van Vechten*. 2 vols. New York: Columbia University Press, 1986.

Cabanne, Pierre. *Le Siècle de Picasso*. 4 vols. Paris: Denoël/Gonthier, 1975–79.

Chipp, Herschell B. "Letter to Emile Bernard," 15 April 1904, p. 19; 25 October 1905, p. 22. *Theories On Modern Art*. Berkeley: University of California Press, 1973.

Daix, Pierre. *Picasso*. New York: Praeger, 1965.

DeKoven, Marianne. *A Different Language Gertrude Stein's Experimental Writing*. Madison: The University of Wisconsin Press, 1983.

Dubnick, Randa K. *The Structure of Obscurity: Gertrude Stein, Language, and Cubism*. Urbana: University of Illinois Press, 1984.

Fifer, Elizabeth. "Guardians and Witnesses: Narrative Technique in Gertrude Stein's *Useful Knowledge*." In Michael Hoffman's *Critical Essays on Gertrude Stein*. Boston: G. K. Hall, 1986.

Four Americans in Paris. Introduction by Margaret Potter. Essays by Douglas Cooper, Lucile M. Golson, Irene Gordon, Ellen B. Hirschland, and Leon Katz. New York: Museum of Modern Art, 1970.

Gallup, Donald. *The Flowers of Friendship: Letters Written to Gertrude Stein*. New York: Alfred A. Knopf, 1953.

Guirand, Félix, ed. *New Larousse Encyclopedia of Mythology*. Introduction by Robert Graves. New York: Prometheus Press, 1973.

Harding, Esther. *The Way of All Women*. New York: Harper Colophon Books, 1970.

Hemingway, Ernest. *By-Line: Ernest Hemingway*. Edited by William White. New York: Charles Scribner's Sons, 1967.

——. *A Moveable Feast*. New York: Bantam, 1969.

Hoffman, Michael J. *The Development of Abstractionism in the Writings of Gertrude Stein*. Philadelphia: University of Pennsylvania Press, 1965.

———. *Gertrude Stein*. Boston: Twayne Publishers, 1976.

———. *Critical Essays on Gertrude Stein*. Boston: G. K. Hall, 1986.

Jackson, Laura Riding. "The Word-Play of Gertrude Stein." In Michael Hoffman's *Critical Essays on Gertrude Stein*. Boston: G. K. Hall, 1986.

Katz, Leon. "The First Making of *The Making of Americans*." PhD thesis, Columbia University, 1963.

———. "Matisse, Picasso and Gertrude Stein." *Four Americans in Paris*. New York: Museum of Modern Art, 1970.

Knapp, Bettina L. *French Novelists Speak Out*. Troy, New York: Whitston Press, 1976.

Luhan, Mabel Dodge. *Intimate Memories*. 4 vols. New York: Harcourt, Brace. Vol. 2: *European Experiences* (1935). Vol. 3: *Movers and Shakers* (1936).

Mellow, James R. *Charmed Circle: Gertrude Stein and Company*. New York: Praeger, 1974.

Meyers, Jeffrey. *Hemingway: A Biography*. New York: Harper and Row, 1985.

Miller, Rosalind. *Gertrude Stein: Form and Intelligibility*. New York: Exposition Press, 1949.

Read, Herbert. *A Concise History of Modern Painting*. New York: Praeger, 1954.

Reid, B. L. *Art by Subtraction: A Dissenting Opinion of Gertrude Stein*. Norman: University of Oklahoma Press, 1958.

Rogers, W. G. *Gertrude Stein Is Gertrude Stein Is Gertrude Stein: Her Life and Work*. New York: Thomas Y. Crowell, 1973.

Rubin, William, ed. *Cézanne: The Late Work*. New York: The Museum of Modern Art, 1977.

Ryan, Betsy Alayne. *Gertrude Stein's Theatre of the Absolute*. Ann Arbor: U.M.I. Research Press, 1984.

Scheff, Aimée. "Theatre of Broadway," *Theatre Arts*, February, 1952. In Ryan, Betsy Alayne, *Gertrude Stein's Theatre of the Absolute*. Ann Arbor: U.M.I. Research Press, 1984.

Schmitz, Neil. "Gertrude Stein as Post-Modernist: The Rhetoric of *Tender Buttons*." In Michael Hoffman's *Critical Essays on Gertrude Stein*. Boston: G. K. Hall, 1986.

Sevareid, Eric. *Not So Wild a Dream*. New York: Atheneum, 1976.

Sprigge, Elizabeth. *Gertrude Stein: Her Life and Work*. New York: Harper & Bros., 1957.

Stein, Leo. *Appreciation: Painting, Poetry, and Prose*. New York: Crown Publishers, 1947.

———. *Journey into the Self: Being the Letters, Papers, and Journals of Leo Stein*. Edited by Edmund Fuller. New York: Crown Publishers, 1950.

Steiner, Wendy. *Exact Resemblance to Exact Resemblance: The Literary Portraiture of Gertrude Stein*. New Haven: Yale University Press, 1978.

Stephens, Robert O. *Hemingway's Nonfiction: The Public Voice*. Chapel Hill: University of North Carolina Press, 1969.

Steward, Samuel M. *Dear Sammy: Letters from Gertrude Stein and Alice B. Toklas*. Edited and with a memoir by Samuel M. Steward. Boston: Houghton Mifflin Co., 1977.

Stewart, Allegra. *Gertrude Stein and the Present*. Cambridge, MA: Harvard University Press, 1967.

Stimpson, Catharine R. "The Somagrams of Gertrude Stein." In Michael Hoffman's *Critical Essays on Gertrude Stein*. Boston: G. K. Hall, 1986.

———. "The Mind, the Body, and Gertrude Stein." In Harold Bloom, *Modern Critical Views: Gertrude Stein*. New York: Chelsea House, 1986.

Sutherland, Donald. *Gertrude Stein: A Biography of Her Work*. New Haven: Yale University Press, 1951.

Testimony against Gertrude Stein. transition, 23. The Hague: Servire Press, February 1935.

Thomson, Virgil. *Virgil Thomson*. New York: Alfred A. Knopf, 1966.

———. *The Musical Score*. New York: Alfred A. Knopf, 1945.

Toklas, Alice B. *Staying on Alone: Letters of Alice B. Toklas*. Edited by Edward Burns. New York: Liveright, 1973.

———. *What Is Remembered*. New York: Holt, Rinehart & Winston, 1963.

Vollard, Ambroise. *Recollections of a Picture Dealer*. Boston: Little, Brown, 1936.

Walker, Barbara G. *The Woman's Encyclopedia of Myths and Secrets*. New York: Harper & Row, 1983.

Walker, Jayne L. *The Making of a Modernist: Gertrude Stein*. Amherst: The University of Massachusetts Press, 1984.

Weinstein, Norman. *Gertrude Stein and the Literature of Modern Consciousness*. New York: Ungar, 1970.

Wilder, Thornton. "Four in America." In Harold Bloom's *Modern Critical Views: Gertrude Stein*. New York: Chelsea House Publishers, 1986.

Wilson, Edmund. *Axel's Castle*. New York: Farrar, Straus & Young, 1952.

Index

193